Eleanor Stuart Patterson Childs, Eleanor Stuart Patterson Childs

Stonepastures

Eleanor Stuart Patterson Childs, Eleanor Stuart Patterson Childs
Stonepastures
ISBN/EAN: 9783743343733
Manufactured in Europe, USA, Canada, Australia, Japa
Cover: Foto ©ninafisch / pixelio.de

Manufactured and distributed by brebook publishing software (www.brebook.com)

Eleanor Stuart Patterson Childs, Eleanor Stuart Patterson Childs

Stonepastures

Stonepastures

Stonepastures

BY
ELEANOR STUART

NEW YORK
D. APPLETON AND COMPANY
1895

COPYRIGHT, 1895,
BY D. APPLETON AND COMPANY.

CONTENTS.

CHAPTER	PAGE
I.—A CITY WITHOUT A STREET	1
II.—WEDDING GLOOM	9
III.—THE BLAST RITE	29
IV.—QUARRY THE SCHEMER	57
V.—HOPE AHEAD	71
VI.—A BAD BARGAIN	86
VII.—TROUBLE ACCUMULATES	99
VIII.—QUARRY'S ATTEMPT AT EXPLANATION	111
IX.—BREAKING UP A HOME	120
X.—QUARRY RECKONS WITHOUT HIS HOSTESS	135
XI.—THE STRIKE	149
XII.—THE EYE OF GOD	166
EPILOGUE	175

STONEPASTURES.

I.

A CITY WITHOUT A STREET.

"To know a man well you must learn his city."

THERE are three districts in Soot City : By the Bridge, By the Tracks, and the Stonepastures.

Simeon Quarry—who lived with the Buttes By the Tracks, and who knew more of this story than I do—always began the tale of his town with this phrase, " As way back as '30"; for that was the year when the big birds sitting on the big boulders first watched the strangers with the strings and water levels, and heard the strangers' words.

There abode in the wilderness of those days—for everything was Stonepastures then—a Methodist preacher with a taste for the scripturally obscure. His circuit included the site of Soot City, to which place he gave the name of Padan-Aram, which endures as the county name until to-day.

Among the strange words the birds heard were "ile," "iron," and "smelt-oven." These sounds were each an "open sesame" to hordes of foreign workers, with a proportion of native Americans generalled by Jo Bentley—grandfather of the Bentley whose plant is still the first in Soot City.

In a single lustre there sprang from the arid strip of country confined with treeless hills—"Baldhead Rangers" and "Cleanshorns"—rows on rows of mean houses, containing men and women every year lessening their acquaintance with the world without. Soot City was their cradle, the arena of their endeavour, their deathbed, and their sepulchre.

By the Bridge dwelt foreman, bookkeepers, furnace masters, together with the Bentleys' outdoor servants—for they had a great place now. The son had rowed in the Cambridge boat, the daughters had become Episcopalians and gave great house parties, and the people By the Bridge who knew them best were the lawyer, the doctor, the baker, and the undertaker, who conspired against the rest of humanity as occasion permitted.

Soot City has no street. Instead, it has narrow-gauge tracks, along which the workmen go forth to and return from labour in the empty ore cars. The houses By the Tracks are ranged on either side of them, and are inhabited by mechanics, iron workers, truckmen, freight handlers, and preachers of minor denominations.

Beyond the bridge are the Stonepastures, and beyond these the ore bed, the smelting place, and the nutt and bolt factory. The bridge straddles the tracks so that the highroad may traverse the town, and the narrow gauge runs from the gate of Bentley's Place to the ore bed under the bridge and over the Stonepastures. The tracks are only four miles long, joining the main line at the furnaces.

No townsman ever looked at the sunset, because it went down on the Stonepastures. Every one's sunset was "over there"; and in the mean hovels that stood out sharply to the town gaze in an evening's afterglow dwelt men who had the white-lead poison in their hands, or who had been scorched in a blast, or who, trying to preserve themselves in alcohol, had failed.

The men were hungry and chafed, wrenching themselves from sleep of a morning to a dull day, three parts thirst to one of hunger.

The children went to school and learned to know their parents' mistakes, bringing home bitterness instead of bread. The mothers washed rags in rusty water, prayed and played with the children, or picked up scrap-iron for the men to sell.

Accident and sudden death were about as frequent as night and day. A squeeze between two ore cars, or a tendency to slumber on the tracks after a "cosey of arrack" at Grigg's drinkshop, meant black on some one's door-handle. But the "blast" was the horror that made the women kiss their men with the fervour of the last parting when they went off to work at the ore bed. The blast was not famous for respect of persons. It rarely killed, but its victims were rarely cured. There was a rocky stretch by the ore bed which young Bentley was having blown out for the town reservoir, and the new iron vein backed against it. Scarcely a blast had been managed without some one being thrown to the earth, mangled with jagged stones—"the throw" the men called them. It might be that some one would fall with the shock and find himself thereafter deaf to everything but the "dumb roaring," and such a one would die of what the unlettered Methodist preacher said was "eternal injuries." The very children feared the blast.

There were, however, three things

that Soot City loved: Pay-day, Jarlsen, and the cinder-flare. At night they would pause in their homeward way from drinkshop or chapel or Jarlsen's neat sitting room, and look toward the smelting furnace. And as the blaze jumped into the yawning sky they would bless its fierceness, and look at the houses and tracks standing out clearly, saying along with their good-nights and good-byes, "God's lookin' at cher, Bill!"

For they named the light from the dumped cinder "The eye of God."

II.

WEDDING GLOOM.

"Death doesn't wait for a man to have his laugh out."—*Salt-miners' saying*.

It is hard for people who have never seen places like Soot City to believe in natures like Emma Butte's and August Jarlsen's. In river cities the labouring population may be augmented daily with a load of tramps and paupers who can travel on the river about as cheaply as their own feet can take them. No travel is as cheap as river boating. River fares cost much less than shoes, and no other cities have the shifting masses that the river cities get.

This is not the nature of an inland town whose mine or iron vein is booming. No one leaves it. What is usual with one man may become the common talk of his district, if he be an influence in it. The vice of a member of the town corporation is the sorrow of the county. The men have gained their livelihood at the hands of the town; they nurse their birthplace when its resource is threatened; they work for it. Even as they live by it they die for it.

In feeling Jarlsen was an American; his ideals were American. He went to church soberly, had a bust of Lincoln on his mantel, eschewed labour unions, and gave away a third of the not too princely stipend awarded him by the Bentleys for his position of payman.

For all that, when the native Swedes got very drunk of an evening and, congregating By the Bridge, swore in their high, unearthly voices, he would be much ashamed and wish and even urge them farther. For he too was born in Sweden, and said "y" for "j" even yet, if the men hurried him.

His room was By the Bridge. His wont was to ask the better set, the more American labourers, to his room of an evening. He then, like King David, charmed them with a harp. He would sit in front of the stove on a packing-box covered with pinkish jute, and there play and sing strange, sweet songs about birds and lonely mountains, and kings' daughters and sad forests, and immortality; for these are of the kinds of songs that come from the North.

Jarlsen's generosity was remarkable; for his countrymen are money-getters beyond any non-Semitic people. The knowledge of the value of money is born in them. There is a saying at the ore beds that testifies to this: "A Swede will go farther for a dollar than an Irishman will for a drink."

But when Jarlsen took Emma Butte, in the face of the whole town, the men of his acquaintance marvelled greatly. If he were the man whom Soot City loved, Emma was the woman who ruled it. She "had not the class" that her lover had.

Coming into the city as a child, she had learned the less rough speech of the town labour and taken on herself the somewhat milder manners of the people she now saw. But she had never tried to make a place among them; she lived with her father, plying her odd trade—she was a barber—and making her oddest pennies in another way, as shall be presently set forth.

In the lighter social semblance of their town the Bentleys were paramount. Their doings came to the town ear somehow, and the people followed their lead, if it were a possible thing for them. For example, one of the clerical workers By the Bridge had invented an intrenching tool, a spade, which had been adopted by the army. As a consequence, he was invited to eat at the Bentleys' Place. On his return from the feast he reported to his eager circle that not only had the ground-floor rooms been filled with people, but that Miss Bentley's bedroom looked like an intelligence office, so full was it of the maids of the ladies below.

This detail of magnificence so possessed the minds of the female portion of the inventor's acquaintance that By the Tracks was drawn on for Abigails. Male escort was frowned down completely. One might return from a Soot City revel with a man, but to go with one—if he were not "steady company"—was proof positive that there was no quarter-dollar wherewith to hire attendance. Emma was often retained as lady-in-waiting, and through this curiously pretentious institution met and obtained Jarlsen, as well as her fees.

Quarry boarded in the Butte household. No one knew why. He imposed on them always, and made them uncomfortable with his odd ways and bad tongue. His board was paid intermittently and with recurrent ill will. He was always a stranger and equally an inmate. He had a fashion of rapping at Emma's window (her room was on the ground floor) and complaining to her of slights imposed on him by members of her acquaintance.

She felt him to be the only man life had shown her whose faults were not condoned by a liking for herself.

Every Sunday found her in a leather apron giving Quarry his Sunday morning's dram of sweetened rum in his tea, to keep him quiet through shaving hours. He came from Ryde, Isle of Wight, and drank tea to the memory of his old home, which had long since forgotten him.

Then Emma would get to work. Her apron was of red leather hemmed up with brass-topped nails. It had a pocket lined with tin, where her lather brush was put when she took the razor from under the straps on her left sleeve to stroke a labourer's jowl. Her lips would be pressed together tightly then, her curling hair caught back with a round comb, like a child's. When she lathered she talked and laughed, but when she shaved she was silent.

Jarlsen shaved himself latterly, and no one understood it but Emma. All the men thought she "had a fluke and struck ile, when she was just digging for potatoes." That she, in the exercise of her odd function, should have secured Jarlsen seemed to them a wonderful thing. But it was not.

Emma was a very good woman, and that is just the same as a lady to men of Jarlsen's. make.

He had begun to shave himself the day he felt he loved his barber. The town discovered his feelings the very day he did, and promptly prophesied trouble. "Jest es soon es he felt like marryin' her he should hev broke her into shavin' weekdays, an' 'kep' a clean chin on him all the time," was what every one said.

Of course, in the eyes of her townspeople Emma put on airs also, for she took to going to church. She never went so far as to stand during the singing, for that would have cost her all her trade. No one stands up in the extremely unorthodox Methodist chapel Soot City operatives affect, except those who are converted or those desiring the prayers of converts.

Now, Jarlsen stood always and was never criticised. His friends said he could sing better if he stood. No one ever asked him if this were true, because they were sure he would say it was not. Thus it may appear that Soot City was not religious, except at blast rites and funerals.

Emma's heart grew mellow with his singing as she sat beside him. She loved him dearly, as young women do love the men who enrich their lives; there was a large element of gratitude in what she felt. She never talked as the others talked about their men, for, as was said, she was a very good woman. And so she got the name of being a lady. The others hated her, and most of the men asked her advice and acted on it.

On the eve of her wedding she sat in her white pique wedding dress, listening to the snarl of the country fiddles as they were played for the dancers. They snarled for two reasons: they were not good fiddles and they were not well played.

The bride-elect was not to go into the dancing room—erst kitchen and tonsorial arena—until Jarlsen came and led her thither. He was a little behind his time, she thought, but her serenity remained complete.

There had been yet no clamour of voices and no clatter of feet, going the faster because so near the last dance. She could hear her name and Jarlsen's. One man told how he had gone to pay off the extra men who were to be discharged after the blast by the new vein.

She remembered that Quarry was on that detail as machinist. That made her think it must have been a long job, for Quarry's voice carried wonderfully, and she did not distinguish it among the others in the kitchen. Her mind wandered to the consideration of the capabilities of her shaving apron as a cover for the packing-box her lover sat on when he played. That suggested to her the probability she should never shave again, and that no woman would dare after her marriage to stand in her doorway and say in venomous admiration, "How elegant you shave!" They had done it often heretofore, God knew.

Her window was raised slightly, and some one tapped on the jamb. She turned her head at this usual intrusion. "Come off, Quarry!" she said hotly.

He came in through the window and stood by the door. "It's a real pity Jarlsen's late," he answered. His voice was hard and nasal, the most effective voice for taunts.

"Is he late?" she asked more crossly.

Quarry laughed. "I guess," he said, "you knew he was late before it would have been quite time for him to come. You know the listening heart worries terrible they say, and you ain't got no call to be so high with me. You can hear them girls in the kitchen laughin' at you, same's I do. I guess Jarlsen's getting tired, may-be. He's kinder in demand, seein' he's the only fellow that's kep' his complexion in the whole plant."

Emma grew rather white. "Stop your nasty tongue!" she cried imperatively. "You're always lying! Your face is lying and your eyes can't see straight. You let what people do to me alone, or you'll have business of your own to settle.

If I was a man, and couldn't get a respectable girl to marry me because I was a liar and she hated me, I'd let her alone for shame's sake, when she took up with a man who can tell the truth."

Her voice sounded very loud in her ears as she stopped ; for the two fiddles were still, and there was no talking among the dancers.

Quarry opened the door as if some one had knocked, and looked out. His features acquired a sudden prominence as the colour flew from his face. Fear crept into Emma's eyes while she looked at him, shaking with his shadow on the half-open door.

She forgot him in the great cry that burst from the other room. It was a horrified, helpless cry, that gave place to a shocked silence.

She wrenched the door back and stood on the threshold in her white, scant gown of mechanic's bride's finery. Her attitude showed faintness, and her head hung down for lack of courage.

The two fiddlers were kneeling, with their tears streaming like rain; they were Polacks, and knelt in gratitude for any excitement. The other men were hushed and stern.

On the big table where the arrack punch had been in company with the less heady beer there was a long, writhing hummock, covered with burlap.

No form was discernible, but Emma knew at the first strong

heart-beat that it was Jarlsen, singed and crippled with a careless blast, as many another had been.

The women wailed at her, and the men tried to stay her with their rusty hands. Yet she went forward, pity for him drawing her, and did not pause until she looked him in the face.

It was black. The hair was gone; his teeth were fixed in the cracked lower lip, and the eyes, once so wide and bold, were pinkish seams beneath the puffed-out temples.

The women had crowded to her back. Their breathing was heavy and in unison.

Emma leaned over him and said softly, in a mother's voice, " Do you hear me speak?" She raised his head on her arm, but it settled back on the table with a sharp crack. He had not heard.

She scanned him closely. She had not yet the full sense of this man covered with burlap and disabled; she only knew that it was not death. But now her lower lip jerked down at the corners, though her eyes were dry. The Polack fiddlers drew each a long breath; they saw the crisis of the scene approaching, and were preparing to bellow loudly.

Emma raised her head. "God's name," she said, "he's blasted!"

The women's faces were curious, inquisitive; and Quarry stood at her side sobbing like a Polack.

The men who had lifted the Swede in after the blast raised him again, and laid him on the bed in Emma's room.

III.

THE BLAST RITE.

"Sometimes if you make ready for bad luck it doesn't come."

No one in Soot City was surprised at a funeral for a man yet in the flesh. Such rites were a custom in the terrible, black little town, where the birds flew low for the damp of steam and the prevalence of soot in the air, and where any fine man who took life eagerly in the morning might be blasted at the noontide snack.

The Scandinavian labourers gave

a tone to all the customs of the town, as the Polacks gave an intensity to all its dissipations. The drink of expatriated Poland is crude alcohol and water, and their drunkenness is a restless insanity that would be murderous in a less childish people. One idea that is directly referable to the Swede minds is that which gave rise to the blast rites. Their feeling had become general that a man might "get beyond the blast"—that is, get over its scorch and shock—if only his friends could be brought to behave as if he were really dead.

Emma was more than Norse in her superstitious observances. She would put a handful of soil from her bit of garden into her wedding shoes, just like any tow-headed bride in the Swede quarter. This was called "getting the favour of home." It was very solemn, and often followed by hysterics.

But the circumstances of Jarlsen's mishap favoured the idea of complete death. He had left a paper with his landlord, "Wavering Jim," providing for Emma in case of "death, accident, or blast." It wasn't a legalized proceeding, but the ignorance of Soot City respected writing beyond most things, and no one would dispute a paper with names signed to it. The three hundred dollars coming thus yearly to Emma would mean a great deal of comfort to her.

The blast rite was to be at Emma's house, as Jarlsen's body was as much an essential to it as if there could have been a sequent interment. The men came in and out a good deal and whispered as to how to tell Emma of her legacy, for every one felt it would be unbecoming to force the news on her. The way in which they broke it to her would have been tactful even for gentlemen.

Wavering Jim came down the tracks in an ore car that sided by the Buttes's gate every night. He didn't get out of it, but waved his hand to her. Emma guessed that he wanted to say something in private, and went to the gate to hear it. "Well," he said, "the weather ain't stopped bein' fine, cert'in'y."

Emma knew it must be something very important to call for a preamble as ornate as this remark about the weather.

Jim paused and looked about him. "Quarry ain't in," said Emma instinctively. "Emma," he said, "I'm stone sure you're frettin' yourself into a terrible chafe 'bout gettin' Mr. Jarlsen proper accommodations, regardin' soup, soft victual, and invalid's board generally."

The girl's eyes bulged with apprehension. "We don't want no subscription papers for us, and if Miss Bentley sends her soup here I'll water the flowers with it. We ain't no Stonepasture poverty yet, to drink the dishwater outer By the

Bridge kitchen. He can't eat nothing but what I get and cook."

"Now jest dry up, Emma Butte," said Jim very gently; "old sheep Bentley with her soup and her weepin' ain't goin' to come soothin' and scratchin' 'round this yard. Jarlsen left a little paper with me that fixes that. All that you've got to do is to practise your signature on his papers in the presence of a few old friends. He grabbed considerable 'fore he was taken," said Jim sympathetically. Leaving the car, he walked nimbly down tracks. No one understands the Godsend news is, in a labouring community. Jim felt elated that he had lodged a man who had money to look after. This vicarious business transaction was the biggest in his life.

Then the undertaker called that evening. He made the same announcement. Small and sympathetic, he threw a cheerfulness into all his sombre doings. He was a rarely lovely man, and had as little jealousy as a sleeping child. He attended blast rites where he never made a penny, as faithfully as he did funerals whereby he supported himself and his friends.

His family were four striped cats. He was extremely fond of prayers and hymns, and, consequently, women. The men never guessed it of him. They knew that he would lend money, but had not yet discovered that, had they been able to repeat a sacred stanza, they need not have repaid him.

Emma's heart beat fast with gratitude when Jeremy Black kissed her. She felt all along that one of the women might have done so, and it added to her uneasiness about Quarry's visiting, for he would look at her and smile, and then wag his shaggy head, as he had always done when he had been about the Tracks telling lies.

She held little, black-coated Jerry very close to her, as disappointed children hug the family cat or dog. The day before she had gone in to kiss Jarlsen, but his poor face was sore with scorch and his side was bruised from where the blast threw him. So she had spread her longing hands over him in realization that the women wouldn't love the barber and that her man couldn't see her sorrow.

Jeremy was immensely pleased with her. He came soon to the subject of the blast rite, and arranged it in his deprecating way, holding his barber's brown hand against his side and calling her Jarlsen's love names, but in a safe, motherly voice that made Emma sure she need not fear the women even if they saw her with him. "Now, Emma, you can't get a regular preacher to pray over anything but a sure and cold corpse, so we'll get Quarry to say the sermon, alludin' to past virtues and the future crown. It'll make things right with Quarry, who ain't the Tracks' darling just exactly, and I'll take the prayers myself. Then the Polacks will fiddle and I'll sing 'The land beyond the sky' and 'Peace comes after pain'—that's a nice song, perfectly novel, with three acts and a chorus. I won't let on it has a chorus, for them Polacks is so insaturated with alcohol they might get things noisy."

"But do speak good and loud," said Emma, "for August might hear something to please him."

"That's right," said Jerry, "don't you lose your grit. You kin never tell how far a man will get beyond the blast with good nursing."

Every one knew that Jarlsen was

stone-deaf since the blast, and Emma spoke of his hearing the—in one sense—post-mortem eulogies from a desire to combat the idea. Perhaps Jeremy feared she might appeal to him for encouragement on this point, for he hurried on to the next.

"Since the beloved lips is silent, I expect I'm the first singer in the city. He had a way of doing gargles on the upper notes that would beat a seraph singing. But I'm goin' to organize as notional a rite as I can, bringing forty years of experience, man and boy, to bear on this one sad occasion. It'll be the blasted best blast rite ever you saw. It's queer they can't cover them blasts or get the men off in time, or so's they won't touch the torch to it before the word's given! I've had some corpses in two years from blasts, and all jest es ragged and singed es could be, let alone the blasts that's lying deaf and blind round the city yet!"

The day of the mock-death service dawned clear and bright, which was held to be bad by the weather-weird-wise, as the Scotch among them said. Quarry had rum in his tea as early as 6 A. M. He was always up early on rum days, but he beat his own precedent this morning.

He insisted upon setting the house in readiness. He had formed a habit of talking to himself since he had grown fearful of committing himself with talking to the other men, for Quarry had many things to hide, and knew his limitations as regarded discretion. His main thought was that he would rather spend money on what was only an approach to Jarlsen's corpse than hoard it. Besides that, he had the cosy consciousness that it had looked friendly when he and Emma had issued together from her room on the night when Jarlsen came singed to his wedding dance.

"The greatest thing happened me since my first drink," he kept saying like a refrain, as he cut long festoons of coloured paper to hang about the mantel and the thinly gilt picture frames. He went By the Bridge to Jarlsen's old room, which was still in some confusion, with his working clothes tossed aside by Wavering Jim. Jarlsen had folded them neatly when he had donned his wedding suit to go pay off the men. It was Jarlsen's portrait in crayon that Quarry had come for. He tied it up with a lank bow-knot of cheap *crêpe*, and laughed in real mirth.

"Now, Jarlsen," he said in banter, "I do seem to see myself somehow in the glass over your portrait. Funny, ain't it?"

By the Bridge he purchased five sticks of pretzels, for in Soot City long sticks are run by venders through these open-work wares.

When all was ready at the Buttes's, he helped lift the big Swede from Emma's cot to the kitchen table. He was dressed, of course, in what was to have been his wedding suit, and the odd lengths of hair that were left him were brushed out on either side of his head to make a good show. His beard had not grown on one cheek, and Quarry surveyed him with great satisfaction. "Seems they've kind o' singed them right-hand glands where the hair starts out," he said. "It's real hard to keep your complexion right here."

Emma had been sleeping on a couple of ironing boards laid on the hard clay of the lean-to where the pans and scant house-tackle were kept. The thought of hardship had not occurred to her. She had saved her heartbroken minutes for the sordid privacy of the chill lean-to. The place had for her the charm of liberty, which, we are told, is the charm of paradise itself.

Her behaviour was not very agonized. She crouched on the blanketed boards and courted the slow tears that crept from her eyes and were healing to her hurt. They alone relieved her; and sometimes, when they would not come, she would grip the scant old skirt that covered her and pray in a loud whisper, with the vital faith of the poor.

When she woke on the morning of the blast rite they had already moved Jarlsen. He lay on the table, roused, but baffled by the strange dimness in him. No voices and no light could come into his world except through memory; he was heir to a limitless pain in the sense of tyrannic suppression that possessed him.

Etiquette assigned Emma the place by the stove. She took it at once as the mourners were gathering rapidly. The company at the wedding dance was indistinguishable in the crowd of to-day.

There were many operatives and all the foremen—of the new vein, the nutt, and bolt factory, etc. These last had their clerks in attendance. Miss Bentley came among the first arrivals, bringing Emma sweet crackers and a hymn-book.

And Emma cursed her—a great,

ignorant, insolent, heartfelt curse—because she thought these things could console her; things the Misses Bentley would never offer each other if their men had the blast. But Miss Bentley was one more of those devout women, not a few, who, because of a congenital shyness, can not do a kindness kindly. Emma would have given thanks for the same things given another way.

The foremen also brought their wives, worthy women with sleek children, who consumed many pretzels with a brisk crunching that annoyed Emma greatly. She wanted people to be sad and unable to eat; to be upset with the trouble that had faded out her future with one too vivid moment of pain.

Quarry sat at a table that was covered with a white cloth. Upon this lay a Bible and a bound time-table. The fitness of this was in the binding, which was ecclesiastically purple.

The table was flanked by the Polacks, looking wretched, as if they had wept all night and grieved since morning on empty stomachs. They tuned their fiddles with writhing faces, and played the "Land o' the Leal," as the remaining space in Emma's kitchen was being filled with the less shy among the labourers. The others stood at the open windows where the sunlight should have been.

Jeremy Black offered prayer, shyly enough, for the Methodist minister was attending as a layman. He prayed for this and that, rather inconsequently, and with a red face; but Emma liked it better than anything else in the service. It was like her own prayer of last night: "O Lord, thou knowest what I want and what I don't want. Please don't send me what I don't want. Good-night." Even to God Emma could not name Jarlsen's death.

Her father came in at the climax of Jerry's petition. He shook his head at Jarlsen's big, quiet shape on the table, and announced in a voice that shook with emotion that "young men would be young men." No one but Emma was galled with this needlessly irrelevant statement. In the less book-learned phases of life many people use expressions just because they admire them, not because they express their feeling, their fancy, or a fact. It is no more to be wondered at than the prayers they make, which would read like telegraphic messages in a High Church congregation.

After his prayer Jerry sang. It is confessed that he sang less for art than for audience. He loved to sing. His voice was thin and rather sweet; his intonation very sure and happy. He contrived to infuse a wistfulness into the most martial or condemnatory ballads, types of song he particularly affected.

There is always a good deal of preface to singing like his, and he was not above throat-clearing and loud swallowing. The verse he sang had been used at blast rites since the Swedes came first to Soot City. Its refrain was sung softly by every one to an accompaniment of rocking bodies:

> "Don't fret, old wife, nor cry,
> For God won't pass you by;
> He may come late, but if you wait,
> You'll get behind the sky."

Then Quarry rose with some pomp and spoke thus: " Ladies and friends: Some lives is all chair-cars and champagne; some lives is neither. I'm not saying what they are, for this is no time to start more tears. Some feels the whip, some wears the willow, some gets their own way. These last says the skimpiest 'Glory be to God!'

"This house is a house of mourning. The one ewe lamb went to the pasture, and come home bit by the wolf! Here to-day, there to-morrow! Our God is a very fearful thing!"

Quarry was considered an orator in Soot City. He always spoke at social functions and stirred his audiences.

"This man"—here the blackest Polack snorted like the report of firearms, and every one at the sound burst into weeping—"this man," screamed Quarry, strengthening his effect, "was a good man! He knew ten at night as well as the town clock. He was a Christian gentleman, and done as well by his friends as he did by the chapel, and what more can a man do? In passing out, those that knowed him good, or any of the men that were pretty common with him, can put their hands on his hand, as some has the feelin' it's best."

Thereupon Quarry made way for himself to the kitchen table, and stood striving against a triumph so strong that it seemed a physical sensation. And Jarlsen lay scorched, inert, and blasted.

To any one knowing the old Saxon custom of touching a corpse as a means of finding its unconfessed murderer the scene would have been more intense from the moment that the first hand—a woman's—was laid on the least sore member of Jarlsen's wrecked body.

None but Miss Bentley knew that the custom was a primitive habit of the race. She alone had a vision of spurting blood as the guilty hand touched its victim. That vision was usual to her at the blast rites, and she felt a strange thrill of uncertainty when she put her own innocent, helping hand on a blasted labourer.

The greater part of the crowd strolled off, subdued, into the bright morning. The rest lingered to lay hands on an old friend.

Jarlsen, the man who had given

his ear to their sorrows and lent his high, searching voice to all their social joys, was virtually dead to them; and it was in tense silence that the heavy-footed workmen approached the table. Then there would be a sobbing sigh, and some one would pass out at the door. Few people can touch the dead without tears, and as Jerry Black said, "The blasts is dead men with live tongues."

They had all gone; the room grew light as the crowd moved from the windows. Sunlight bathed the floor at Emma's feet, and Black stood beside her, knowing she feared to be without him when Jarlsen was deaf to her and Quarry spoke his kind of love to her, and her father was only a peevish old child. Quarry laid a nervous hand on Jarlsen, who had been roused more than once through his tactile sense as some old friend's hand had lain for a moment on his.

When Quarry's touch fell on him, he cried out, "O Emma, Emma! am I dead, that I can not hear you? Is your voice gone behind the sky, that you hold your mouth yet? Is your hand cut off you? Don't marry Quarry till I am home again! Emma, tell me where you are. It is all black inside me!"

Emma leaped to him. She was "swift as a wicked cat," Quarry told her later on when he cursed her.

She hurt him cruelly, but Jarlsen

smiled, and his blackened face grew brighter. "I shall not marry until Heaven—" she vowed, but he could not hear. The pain of her embrace was fearful, but she clung fast, and called out in her big voice the loyalty he longed for and that he felt in the suffering her strong arms caused him, even though he could not hear.

And then Jerry touched her. "I'm afraid he's fainted," he said, as though he apologized.

IV.

QUARRY THE SCHEMER.

"The winged word of spite outstrips a kindness."

EMMA was too tired to feel her unhappiness, and too relieved, now that everything was over, to feel her loneliness very much. The blast rite had somehow robbed her of her hope of Jarlsen's recovery, and established the idea of his death in her mind. Jeremy Black nursed him at first, after her outburst. In the neighbours' phrase, he "turned and fed the poor blast."

Emma's crude nature found a pleasure—never before known to her—in food, and in lying on the lean-to floor and thanking God that her barber days were over. Her voice was harsh and loud; she had always hidden it from Jarlsen. To-day she sang and was not ashamed.

Then Black went mysteriously to the city. This might mean New York, Pittsburg, Philadelphia, or some nearer, smaller town than either of these. He left at the beginning of the drought, and Emma, with the rest of his townspeople, envied him sorely. Her resumed service to Jarlsen was automatic. He spoke, but she did not listen; she was afraid of being hurt if she heard his words. The drought made her double work, for her patient drank a great deal of water, and refused it with a wearied patience if it were not cold. She often went at noon to the Bridge well, her tin dipper growing burning hot beneath a sun that made the mica specks shine in the roadside dust. She lagged heavily down the hill, the people greeting her and she answering without knowledge of what they said. She had learned that forgetfulness is the better part of wisdom.

She could not ignore Quarry; he was merciless. On Sunday she went at six for Jarlsen's drink from the well. She had a handful of oatmeal to put in it; and, as she leaned over and caught the dripping bucket, she heard Quarry's voice in the alder thicket that smelt sweet with the heavy dew on it.

"She's a real good girl, and I can't help but feel, ef she could let me at her wedding dance, set alone with her waitin' till Jarlsen come, that I owe it to her to marry her, and I think when she's worn out her mourning thet she'd be agreeable. He was a queer fellow; hed them fancy virtues thet prevents a man from making a good husband jest as sure as his havin' the vices would. He give his money to lame-legged and blind-eyed, and thet's keepin' it from wifie jest es much es if he give it up for drink."

A woman's voice answered him in full assent: "You'll not be the only one to marry her, though; she's got money now, and a rare head for livin' straight."

Emma had not seen the woman, but guessed it must be one of those who "wrought" in the offices of the plant, writing, or sorting the mass of mail. Excepting herself Quarry rarely spoke to any one of less class among the women.

She was very angry, and could see how Quarry had used it all in his talk; all the circumstances of her courtship he could twist into evidence that she had loved nothing of Jarlsen but what he had left her. She could hear the woman's opinion that her conduct was not quite right, uttered in the dry tone she used when speaking of her straight life.

She said to herself just as fiercely as ever that Quarry was a liar, but she felt that happiness had given her the power to fight him, and now her happiness was gone. She remembered with a dim horror that Quarry had resumed a practice, since Jarlsen's mishap, that she hoped her engagement had ended. Up to the day that they had spoken of their marriage publicly, Quarry would take things into his hands that Emma had lately touched and fondle them. He had done so again the day of the blast rite, she remembered.

She had intended to revel in her grief at chapel that morning, and

Quarry had divined her intention. She meant to stand in the singing, as Jarlsen had stood, and sob when the preacher shivered and scowled and beat the reading-desk with his fists. She would not go now. She felt that no one would believe that she mourned for him if Quarry had been talking about her very much in the way she had heard. She burned to speak with him of the traitor's part he had played.

It was as usual in Soot City as in other places for folks to bethink themselves of the church when trouble thwarts them; and so every one went to church expecting Emma. And Quarry's tongue was not quite long enough to have reached the general ear in so short a time.

The congregation was very large, and the flattered minister observed Emma's absence with satisfaction. He never thought that his hearers could have been ignorant of her intention to stay at home, and supposed that in the sudden calamity come upon the town they had found a warning anent churchless ways. He announced an extra service at three in the afternoon, and the only person who answered it was Jeremy Black's foreman, who came to protest.

After service Quarry went straight to Emma's room. He could not account for her absence; he had intended to sit with her in the front pew while she stood in the singing. He expected to colour his stories with her behaviour and satisfy every one that she had loved the money Jarlsen left her the best of all his attentions.

She was sitting with her charge, who lay with his face turned away from the sun—blind, maimed, deaf —yet as conscious of Quarry's presence as when last week he had turned to him with lazy scorn and a short word.

"Emma," said Quarry.

"Yes," she said, after a pause. She had been wondering if he could have been telling about the money everywhere and "setting the men on her."

Quarry looked at her and at Jarlsen with a twist in his mouth that he thought of as "his smile." He realized that he could insult Emma thoroughly in the presence of a Soot citizen who could not stir to protect her.

"The women think you might as well marry," he said. "You've got the fixin's, and if you take me you've got the husband. The whole place expects a wedding off you. You've got the extra money to care for your friend here."

"I'd rather give up the money than take you; besides," she said spitefully, "there's better men nor you in the town that knows I have money for my man. You ain't no kind to love me after what I've had, and I don't want you should make my love for this one shabby, talkin' it over all the time. You can get out," she said very quietly.

Quarry went; and, as he said himself, his heart was sour.

Then Emma stayed at Jarlsen's side and prayed in the hot afternoon silence, and wondered why God didn't do something worth while—that is how she thought it. But she never doubted Him nor the fate that He ordained, but rocked in her only rocking-chair and kissed her helpless lover boldly, longing for a woman's touch as a sick child longs for its mother.

When Jarlsen spoke her name she trembled with love of him; she was awake now and filled with pity. She did not answer, but, like a child, prayed God to tell Jarlsen she heard him call, and then slept till the coolness of dusk awoke her. Jarlsen slept a little while too, and told her he had talked with her in dreams.

She got the supper, talking within herself. "I can feel things mend," she said. "Every one will come out right, and my big man will live again and lick that terrible scant Christian, Quarry!"

She ate her supper opposite her silent old father. It was quite late; they had candles and a lamp, which was only an extravagance for courting-time in the sordid social usage of Soot City.

Emma had not thought of this till Ben Bowa, the youngest foreman, stood in the narrow doorway.

"I didn't know to come in till I

saw lights making the shine," he explained in Swedes' English. And then many more came in, and the kitchen was full. Jarlsen cried for water from the next room, and before Emma could get to her feet Quarry had gone to him.

"How can I show them I don't want one of them?" she thought. There was no word of Jarlsen, and everything went on as it had when the one or two men courted her before Jarlsen took her.

Bowa cut profiles out of paper and asked whose they were, and the other men performed their trifling social accomplishments. They were endeavouring to "raise a laugh"; none came.

Late at night a wakeful neighbour heard Emma's door close, and later God heard her sobbing. "That Quarry's done me!" was what she said.

And through the night her eyes burned, and she felt that the darkness fell like a weight on them. She longed even for Miss Bentley or the Polack girls' overdressed Madonnas.

V.

HOPE AHEAD.

"Only the saints and the feeble-minded suffer gladly."

EMMA tossed restlessly that night. Once the cinder flare leaped upon her walls, staining them with a flickering orange glow. This incident emphasized to her mind the horrid blackness that had lately fastened on their household.

She awoke very early next morning in the final, nervous way that worried people dread, and sat huddled on the floor of the lean-to in the still, sunless cold. Jarlsen's loud talk echoed in the empty kitchen, but she knew she could not wake him with her voice. The thought recurred to her with all the force of discovery that, waking or sleeping, the voices of this world were dead to him.

Black would return to-day. It was odd to call this hour to-day. The noontide that would bring Black again to Soot City seemed very different from any dim time of loud agonies like that which makes the dawns of the sore-hearted.

To-day she would also be paid the "blast money," part accident insurance and part Jarlsen's savings. The anticipation of this pleased her until she moved into the disordered kitchen and saw the chairs as Bowa and the others had left them, and smelt the lamp that was a survival of the courting days she had prized. Then she groaned.

For a moment the idea of bringing out the leather barber's apron and the keen razors, as a tacit contradiction to any report of her wealth, seemed a clear inspiration. But with Quarry and Wavering Jim to talk, she knew all delicate denial to be useless.

She opened the house and sat along the narrow door-sill, her back to one jamb, her knees drawn up and fixed against the other. As the sun came up, the cinder flare crept in a stealthy flush along the earth and lost its power in the heavens as the day grew bright.

At last the cold stung her hands, and the sun chased the shivers down her back, so that she went again into the house, forgetting that an hour since she had loathed it. Quarry was with Jarlsen, who clamoured on, asking questions whose answers he could not hear.

He was learning his deafness by degrees, for his fits of silence were longer, but with Quarry he talked always. Quarry's touch was abominable to the Swede, and his presence pricked to the quick a soul whose every other approach was blockaded.

Emma, in pity, took up the jug of sweet oil to bathe the burns.

Her hand was light from shaving, and it had learned a wonderful caution from the teachings of pain. She could mitigate its brown strength with a suddenness like the swift softnesses of Jarlsen's old-time singing, and he would smile at her as she used to smile at his own skilled tunefulness. She almost stroked the scorches with her wise, soothing hands.

She had meant to spend the morning on the doorsill, in the hope that a passing woman might be kind and glance her way. She longed so for a woman's friendship! She was sure that half the sting of her sorrow would vanish with recital.

At the last accident, when they

brought home Jerry Black's half-sister's husband from a squeeze between the ore cars; as soon as every one had made quite sure he was dead, Martha Long—herself a personage even in the presence of a newly made widow—caught Jerry's sister in her arms and rocked to and fro with her standing, until both women fell on the plush sofa.

Such scenes dignify sorrow in one type of the common mind.

Emma knew that Quarry had lied about her, and through the day she wondered what the lie might have been. The absence of feminine condolers worried her, and added to her dread of the time when the hands of the clock should reach half past one. That was the hour of Jarlsen's leave-taking on the day before that set for their wedding. As the time approached the ticking of the clock seemed louder, and she went into the lean-to to escape from it. She lay there, covered over and quiet as though night had come.

The latch rattled, and Martha Long, with her thin face and burning eyes, stood in the lean-to doorway with her baby's half-knit hood in her fingers. She cast a glance of piercing inquiry at Emma, and her emphasis was not conciliatory.

"Well," she said, "God has strange ways with the righteous. You've had your troubles, poor girl!"

"I don't see there's need for that

kind o' talk," said Emma vaguely; "them as gives it ain't had overmuch, I guess!"

"Well, no offence," said Martha, overbearingly; "how is he?"

"Making out—no more. He ain't got a piece of skin on him that don't appear to be fried, and he talks till your heart splits in your body."

"It's a good sign if he's rebellious. My brother was fearful meek. He could hear a little, and the whole town had hopes, when one morning he turned his head in to the wall, and he says to poor Jarlsen, who was tending him, 'You give that oatmeal and water where it's wanted,' he says; 'you can give me a pleasure drink for the last I get.' He didn't drink much ever, and Jarlsen give him a drop of something, and then he lay still and was dumb dead before your poor feller could rinch the glass. So it goes!" Martha ended dismally.

Emma did not find this quite satisfactory, so she said nothing.

"And there is something you have to be thankful for," said Martha further, forgetting that nothing causes man to hate his lot like telling him to be thankful for it; "you've got a good man to fall back on. That Quarry's more to you in most ways nor your born mother would be. Yesterday he was saying as how risky it was to marry where the language was different. Two tongues like that in a house means secrets."

Emma had started up. "That Quarry says more than his prayers," she cried out fiercely; "I knew he'd been lyin' 'round about me. I don't hold by his ways; and I'm goin' to stick by that husk of a husband in there, ef he don't get better till the day I die. He ain't talked kind about me, and worse talk is due, I know, but I'll bide my rights, and have 'em."

Martha felt admiration. Emma was not as Quarry had reported her. She recited a few more "incidents," and strolled, without leave-making and still knitting, toward the door. "Come in some night when you're lonesome," was all she had left in her heart of the invitation she had meant to give the girl in Bowa's interest. It was plain to her woman's eye that Emma loved Jarlsen maimed better than a town full of men of sound members.

She wondered, however, why the girl hadn't the sense to take Quarry, who was getting in with the factory hands like water through a leak.

Black came in a moment after Martha's departure. He had a wallet in his hand, and his face was clothed in a bright kindliness that turned Emma's heart toward him.

"I'm glad you've had lady's company," he said.

"You're looking daft, dear," Emma answered, when she had studied him.

Suddenly the little fellow spread his hands. "Last night," he said, "I went to heaven cheap—fifty cents entrance fee. I heard a man play on a fiddle; well, if the sweetest voice in heaven sang its best it couldn't learn that feller much. I sat there and just pined away to hear the back door shut, or some other shabby kind of sound, just to show it was really I situated in the concert hall. But that's not this," he concluded, putting his hand on the wallet; "here's your due."

Jerry held it out to her. His face was red, and he made visible efforts to control its expression, which changed from conscious diplomacy to kindly eagerness.

"I seen a doctor in the town, a professor of blasts, kind of. He knows the ins and outs and conbinizations of paralysis pretty pat, and I told him I had a good friend laid up in a blast, and he said he'd charge maybe a hundred or maybe fifty dollars to come up on purpose to see him. So that's your best way of layin' out his money, Emma."

"I was thinkin' that would be good myself," Emma answered with a quiver of gratitude on her lips.

"And I'm obliged to say that you could offer a little to Quarry, just to keep his tongue sweet. He's got a fearful gainin' way with his mouth, and them nutt and bolt hands will pick up and listen to all he has to say. They've been in schools, and are crazy for talkin' and politics. The kind of foolishness men gets from schools is the worst kind."

Jerry was angry.

"Ain't he been talkin' on me, maybe?" Emma asked.

"Perhaps so, perhaps no. He's so mean you could buy him for a small price. He ain't much of a luxury."

As they talked they heard the dinner pails clanking as some of the men came down the homeward hill. Then an oar car sided under the window close by the house. In it were the workmen of the nutt and bolt factory—Quarry in their midst, his face ardently conceited and his gestures highly alcoholic.

Emma scanned him with a fierce contempt. "He wouldn't be like that if he could stir around," she exclaimed, pointing toward her own room door.

Then she stood by Jarlsen's bed to avoid Quarry, and as she looked at him he laughed; it was his old, mirthful, kindly laughter. It seemed to the girl, who cherished him, that he had brought pain to their house, and had also been spared its consequences. She suffered—he slept.

VI.

A BAD BARGAIN.

"It is well to pay your debts, on the chance you'll lose your money."

In four days' time Black received a letter from the paralysis specialist that delighted him. It consisted solely of questions regarding trains and Soot City conveyances and the distance from the station to the patient's abiding place. To the genial undertaker intercourse with a man too busy to con a time-table was social promotion.

He went at once to Emma, and

in a mixed state of reverence and elation read her the physician's curt note, with his own copious comment.

"Sounds 'cute, don't he?" said Black. "He knows I understand him. It must be a kind of comfort to him comin' to a strange place to find a man of his own stamp who feels just his way about the game o' life."

Putting his tongue in his cheek, he was soon lost in wonder to find himself, after long years of comparative obscurity, so very like this shining light of medical science.

Emma almost said her thought aloud; it was well she did not, for she was saying inwardly, "You can always tell when Jerry Black's been to the city, he has such an extra green look."

With Martha Long for aid, she prepared for the doctor joyfully. They washed everything just for the love of the unaccustomed, that seizes women under suspense. Everything had been washed for the wedding, and was still much cleaner than its ordinary state. There was one day when the house-cleaning was finished and the doctor not yet come; so Martha undertook a little rudimentary cooking, and Emma raked up the little space of yard and dug out the weeds from the beds of cinder-spotted marigolds.

She tended Jarlsen more and more, and the friendliness Martha showed toward her pleased her mightily. She would take her to the Swede's bed and show her how his looks were coming back, and then, forgetful of her presence, would stand in silent wonder at the expression of wisdom fast becoming habitual to him.

He seemed to know more of what was, and is, and is to be, than any of the people she had seen, and he had not seemed so wise when he had lips wherewith to speak wisely. For a half hour and more she would sometimes watch him, unconscious of time, and at last a fit of longing, like a mother's, would bend her to him. Anxious for his thoughts, she would put her hand on his temple as if feeling for them. He would smile and say "Emma"; then her blushes would come as they had when he was a bright mystery to her, because she dared not raise her eyes to his face; and she took the utterance of her name as an answer to her craving.

Quarry and her father had become cares she could not shoulder; she simply could not think of them. Quarry never returned from work without company, and he and his friends would sit in the yard on Emma's chairs, which they carried from the kitchen without her permission. In a man she liked, this proceeding might have been annoying; but from Quarry it was a liberty that was enraging.

One day Emma heard him stirring up strife with his tongue; he was a fascinating speaker, even when—as the Swedes said—he "talked beside his mouth," which is their idiom for conversational embellishment.

She called him to her. "Send them away," she said shortly.

Without a word of dissent he made them move, and Mr. Butte shambled out to bring in the chairs.

"Take them in yourself," she called wickedly. "You was strong enough to get them out there."

With a more sullen compliance he put them just within the narrow doorsill.

Still she eyed him with her mouth stretched into something

like a smile. "Put 'em in their places," she said.

Again Quarry obeyed her.

Then her contemptuous smile became laughter. "You wouldn't hev done thet ef you hedn't got wind of what I'm goin' to even to you. See here—you talk too much. Would you talk less if you had more money? I guess maybe. Here's what you said at Martha Long's party. You showed how it was a good thing August Jarlsen got the blast, because I kind o' leaned toward you latterly. And as for you, you says you'd always leaned toward me, and it was better to have August Jarlsen saved learnin' it." The girl covered him with her tragic eyes, and expressed her own strong instinct in a gesture she had learned from the Polacks—she crossed herself with a rapid hand. She had never before felt Quarry to be so evil. "Now," she said, "fifty dollars if you'll stop that!"

For a moment delight leaped from his eyes. He threw out his hand; then he looked at her darkly, his expression altered to one of fear and misgiving.

"All right," he said finally.

"Well, I'll pay you later," said Emma, and every word she spoke cut like a whip, her voice was so shrill with contemptuous anger.

She was a young girl, and had hoped he would not take the money; partly because she didn't wish to believe that he could be mean enough to take it from her, when he knew that he was the last person the Swede would give it to, had he any longer the power to give.

Her lips shrank away from her teeth in contemptuous, writhing smiles when she thought of it.

She scarcely knew how to array herself for the doctor's visit. She wanted to impress him with a sense of her fitness to nurse the patient. She had had visions of Jarlsen's departure in an ambulance for some city hospital, where a uniformed woman would hear his groans and heed them for hire only.

Quarry knew nothing of the doctor's advent. Emma understood that he would talk about it, and that her enemies would say she must be sure of Jarlsen's death when she dared let loose a first-class pill-man on him.

Then, besides, the Englishman was unreasonable and iterative, like many Englishmen; and she knew how he would search his mind for ways to tell her that Jarlsen was as good as dead already. "I ought to pay him right away, or he'll do a little of his fancy talkin', maybe."

Black went to the station in a funeral carriage, which was the more imposing as there were but four in Soot City. (Casually—he paid toll on the turnpike for the eight horses that drew these vehicles, and they were always taxed as "pleasure teams." Again casually—he saw no joke in this, even when the mourners received legacies.) He wore a red tie with his black, professionally sombre clothes, and this he did as he would not imply Jarlsen's death to the doctor, in case the physician should be standing on the platform and should see him before he could get speech of him. Black employed his imagination in this sort of futile arrangement of improbable circumstance.

On the doctor's arrival they drove directly to the Buttes. They alighted at the Bridge and saw thence to Emma's doorway, where Quarry was standing. He looked as though he had had rum in his tea, and as if even that had not reconciled him to existence.

"Where's Emma?" he asked of Black.

"She's in with August. Dr. Brent, this gentleman lives here; he's an old friend of Mr. Butte's, and Mr. Jarlsen's too, I may say."

Quarry, returned in the noon recess to find a perfect stranger about to invade the house; did not understand the situation, as was very evident. He grinned absently, and went toward Jarlsen's room door.

"Emma, come out here." His tone was wheedling, and his fingers were tapping nervously on the wall. She came out to him quickly; her eyes were bright and her face was full of a vigorous hope.

"Hurry up!" she said; "I want to bring the doctor in."

"Could you oblige me with the trifle you named Thursday? I want to blow it right in this noon."

Emma thought it wise to pay him at once, although her heart was beating in her ears — she longed so for the doctor's opinion on Jarlsen. She hesitated, and then said: "It is in the wallet between the shake-downs in the lean-to chamber. Put it back where you found it."

She forgot him as she greeted the doctor; her whole mind was full of the Swede.

VII.

TROUBLE ACCUMULATES.

"If you're feeding a mean dog, be sure he'll bite you when he's had enough."

THE doctor let Emma tell him her own complete narrative of Jarlsen's mishap; nor did he interrupt once, save with questions that served as a spur to her flagging memory. Her mode of recital was detailed and feminine, obnoxious to science. She told, incidentally (but at great length) how Jarlsen had always treated her; and quoted his sayings, which were, in her retrospective judgment, prophetic. The doctor's manner was so courteous that a more experienced girl than Emma could not have inferred that Jarlsen's relations with her before the accident would not strike his physician as indicative of his condition after it.

Dr. Brent had a sober, inscrutable smile; he gave the observer an impression of seeing with great difficulty, although he wore no glasses. His manner was at times indifferent, yet he inspired confidence. As Jerry had said, "He don't have to hustle to cure you, like these farmin' pill-men we hev to Soot City."

Emma was so rapt in the first uninterrupted recital of her troubles that she did not observe Quarry as he crossed the kitchen to the house door. He had the wallet in his hand, which shook; his face twitched and was chalk white.

"I hope that is not your father," said Dr. Brent politely as he would say: "There is a shower coming; I hope it may not wet you."

Emma looked at him and liked him, for she saw that he knew at a glance what Quarry was. And she had taken lessons in him for a lifetime and had not learned him yet. Then the doctor rose and went into Jarlsen's room.

Waiting for the doctor's opinion is one of the fearful things that civilization has imposed on humanity. It is during such intervals of suspense that a racked mind learns the pattern of the carpet, the similarity in outline of some familiar pieces of furniture, and of some impossible beast or bird sprawling on the wall papers. Emma discovered stains in the sheer curtains at the window. She prayed in a general way, and feared the moment when the doctor should appear again.

For the first time she observed that quite a crowd surrounded the house, looking in at the windows. They wore long faces beneath their eager eyes, and looked as though good news would be a (conversational) calamity. Jerry Black, however, stood among them with the perfect aspect of honest sympathy.

It was to him that Emma beckoned. He entered the house in response, with an air of great importance. He had been telling half the town by twos and threes, and as a great favour, exactly what he had said to Dr. Brent. The town listened in the hope of hearing what Dr. Brent had said to him.

Emma motioned him to stand close to her.

"When do you pay?" said she.

"'Most any time," said Jerry. "You can pay the first day for a whole set of visits, or you can pay when he sends a bill, or 'most anyway."

"How can I tell how often he's comin'?"

"He ain't let pass that he's comin' more than this once, but you'll have to go high for this once.

Think of the fares here and back; the car money alone is twenty-five dollars, and not countin' chair-cars or meals."

"Well, I'll give him a hundred, and see how he likes that."

"All right," said Jerry; "you give it to him now. He'd be more likely to come later, if he knew we pay before he can put hat on to go home."

She had planned it all; the money should be put in his hand just as he was leaving. She thought of no receipt, just as she thought of none for the money she put in the plate on those delightful courtship Sundays. Indeed, she felt the transactions to be similar.

She wanted to show, just as she had shown then, that though Jarlsen was her man, he was no pauper. The bill was to be paid in the sight of the surrounding multitude at the windows.

Presently Dr. Brent came out. He looked at the faces set in the window frames, and made no comment. Emma realized, with hope full grown to thankfulness, that had he felt there was nothing encouraging to say, he would have dispersed the waiting men and women before he spoke.

"Miss Butte," he said, "I've seen worse than he recover. His sight is gone, sealed up with scorch; but he'll hear again some day. Get him up as soon as the smart goes."

Some one in the window said, "He'll make wages dead easy if he hears again."

"I'm glad," said Dr. Brent, turning toward the window. "Encourage him to work when the smart is over."

He declined Emma's offered meal, and prepared for departure, writing on a bit of paper what he wished to have done for Jarlsen. When he rose, hat in hand, Emma spoke to him. Her voice had a thrill of pride in it, and her high spirit lent a dignity to the gaudy finery intended to decorate her awkward frock.

"Doctor," she said, "will you set a minute?"

She entered the lean-to, erect and elastic. Three minutes passed while the crowd asked the doctor questions, which he answered in words of such strangeness to their ears that they enjoyed all the sensations of those who communicate with spirits. They laughed at his least word, and he, perceiving it, darkened his sayings the further.

When Emma returned, her face was set and her cheeks flamed, so that their heat alone drew the tears to her eyes. Her hands shook, and hardly held the bit of soiled paper and the stumpy pencil that she carried. "Will you tell me your name and address?" she asked of the doctor.

A sigh broke from her lips that tried not to be a groan.

Black looked at her, and the

colour flew from his face. He said afterward that his heart beat so that he thought some one knocked on the door. He knew what had happened.

So did the doctor. "My accounts are payable in May," he said, being kind, and knowing Soot City to be ignorant.

Emma smiled again, and, with the patronizing manner that is the outcome of complete shyness, said, "Well, you're a real good doctor."

And so, with a slight constriction of his kindly heart, he shook her hand and departed.

But she caught Black at his exit. "That Quarry's stole!" said she.

Jerry looked sick and old; his voice sounded bitter. "I ain't got a cent just now to spare," he said. Then he grew fiercer, and cursed the Englishman exhaustively and with the awkwardness of a man unused to such conversational indulgence.

The crowd followed as far as the funeral carriage and stood to watch it disappear in billows of dust. The white horses and the black barouche were alike buff before they were out of sight of The Tracks.

And in sullen quiet Emma set herself to wait for Quarry, not trusting herself to look at Jarlsen lest the sight of him should soften her hate.

"He took the whole wallet!"

she repeated to herself, "and he was the only man August wouldn't give to. He knew it, too, or he'd hev asked something off him when first he seen we was settin' it up together."

VIII.

QUARRY'S ATTEMPT AT EXPLANATION.

"A man will say more to himself in excuse than he will to his God or his friend."

EMMA'S eyes roved from object to object as though she sought escape; they always returned to the door, whence she expected Quarry. It was a duty, she reasoned, to turn this man's stealing to swift shame. Words flocked to her tongue that she could not remember having used before, and her mind's eye saw the Englishman wince under them. A demon of invective filled her brain with fierce thoughts as she tore the shake-downs apart in a final hunt for the wallet. And then a fit of sobs and shaking beset her as she waited again in the kitchen for what she hoped would be in some sort vengeance.

She remembered every mean and, in her characterizing adjective, every "useless" thing Quarry had done; how he had lied, and when. She remembered his drunkenness—that terrible drunkenness in which his self-assurance seemed boundless; the remembered vanity of his face startled her, and it seemed marvellous that his faults had not kept him from their household as they had kept him from their hearts.

When some person has been the provoking cause of emotions so strong that the mind can not shake off their grasp, it is quick to misconceive that person. Quarry's voice was a shock to Emma when at last she heard it in the yard, although a short time ago she had seen and had speech with him.

Her heart sank when she found he was talking with himself and in a laudatory strain. His effort was to walk straight, but his accomplishment was slight. He lurched to and from either marigold border, so that the walk seemed serpentine to Emma's shocked gaze. "No," he said, "the ruins is covered with ivory; I shall pluck away the vine, and the presspit is discovered." He spoke as he walked, doing as much as possible at each lucid interval between lapses. "No friend shall fall away into the presspit, like I nearly did."

His fall was upon nothing more precipitous than the chair by the door. Seeing anger on Emma's face, he attempted to soothe her with vague smiles of fearful extent; they travelled swiftly across his flushed face and divided it into north and south intemperate zones.

"Stop *that*," called Emma; "you've done enough!"

"Not yet!" shouted Quarry, impelled by an erratic enthusiasm; "I'll do more for my Emma. I've laid out the money real well. We'll buy the deepo and live in it! It's the finest house in Soot City, and if you want Jarlsen too, you can keep him for hired help. I don't want there should be any stinting where love is king."

"Give me my wallet," said Emma.

"I have given it where it'll do the most good. The town rejoices that a good deed was done. Mine the deed though not the money." He used this phrase as a sort of chant.

"Quarry," said Emma sternly, "sober up, and think true for a minute!"

But he interrupted to say: "Sober up? Emma, you're enough to turn a saint. I am so sober that the boys laugh at me the way they done at Jarlsen, and I've done the wonderfullest thing! Money'll be so loose you can pick it up off anything in such a little while! I invested yours in a great concern; it's safe. I'm at the head of it!" He finished, with some tardy regard for truth, and, waving his arms comprehensively, lapsed again into vagueness.

"Where did you put it?" Emma uttered her queries with pains, as if she put them to a foreigner.

Then came lavish excuse. "I put it in an investment," said he. He was a little sobered now, and wore a scared look. "Mr. Jarlsen, 'fore he was took with the blast, got me to promise to invest his money. He had a pulmonition of the blast, so he did."

Emma looked at him again; her

face was white and hopeless, and its young modelling seemed aged and heavy.

"You ain't gone and sunk that altogether, Quarry, hev you? If you hev, there's only the Stonepastures left. It'll be a hard thing to pass the Bridge once for all and see your work-fellers comin' through on the cars, and you only comin' es fur es the Pastures from the factory. Can't you think what you done with it?"

"I've spent it. It's invested—but still—it's spent."

She saw that the men would have to take the matter up for her. At first anger had nerved her, but now she felt weakly despairing. It seemed to her that there was no use in effort to set right circumstances so awry, until, as she said, "things had stopped happening."

"Well, you're a thief, anyway," she said, "and I'd fight you if I had any pith in me!"

Quarry raised himself. "That's you all over," he remarked sadly. "I've seen you leap on Jarlsen quick as a wicked cat; and a lady as lifts a hand to a half-dead man is no lady. You have made my life very profane, Emma. I don't find in you the flavour of a godly woman, Emma Butte," he added with a final effort at dignity. "You're a—a—mean girl!"

Emma rose, and, standing, looked him over thoroughly. No idea of law came to aid her ignorant helplessness. She understood now the saying that women were "put upon." Some girls would have cried, but Emma had one sweet drop in the bitter draught. She would have to move to the Stone-pastures, but by so doing she could pay the doctor, even though she had to shave again.

IX.

BREAKING UP A HOME.

"It is better to live under God's sky than under a roof when there's no luck there."

You and I, knowing the use of pen, ink, and paper, and the efficacy of latter-day postal systems, must remember that there are degrees of education ; also, that all the methods of communication in well organized communities are as unknown to the ignorant, Americo-alien population of such places as Soot City as is the fate of nations to the speculative schoolboy. Emma needed Black's counsel, but she did not think of the post as a means of getting a letter to a man in her own town. She reasoned that post-office people would slight mail matter not destined to go by train to other cities. So her anxious heart kept her waking to catch the light, that she might get away in secret to Black's house and there put her case in his ever-open and ever-busy hands.

Youthful weariness demands sleep. Emma was young and overweary, and, as a consequence, overslept.

It was in the fear that calamity might have stolen another march on her that she dressed herself. She had about her a neatness that enraged the down-at-heel disheartened, of which there are so many in labouring communities.

"The world," she thought, "has thumped me till I ain't got half the spring I hed to start on; and that's the reason I'm goin' to dress up. I'll wear cuffs till I've got to sell 'em, and a collar, ef I do have to shave for a livin'."

But she had not enough pleasure in living left to heat the coffee that her father had used at his breakfast; she was only thankful that he had gone away for his paper By the Bridge, and that she might set about vacating the house, with a will. She did not think of consulting him. When a man has consented all his life to anything and never met any circumstance, crucial or casual, with aught but irrelevant comment, he is rarely a factor in other people's plans.

She was glad she had not had to get breakfast, for she had to tend Jarlsen. The day was wet, and his hurts seemed the sorer for the damp. When she had done all for him she laid her hand on his, but the dread of packing her wedding things was making war on her energies. She felt she could not rest till she had packed the white gown out of sight and mind. Before now she had held a private service of tears over her six wedding presents. Miss Bentley had given her a jacket edged with good fur, and her sister had given her some fine stockings; but her lover's gift meant more to her than any other inanimate thing. It certainly meant more than bread, for she would have starved before she sold it, and died in happiness had her eyes but met it as they closed finally.

It was a large locket of reddish gold, embossed in clumsy arabesque; within were two photographs—of Jarlsen and of Cheyne Falls, where they were to have spent their wedding week. It was the fashionable tribute from groom to bride in Jarlsen's circle of Soot citizens, and Emma felt that with this gift he conferred his higher class on her. It was just what he would have given the first foreman's daughter. She opened the locket and looked in. Eve may have felt like her and Emma thought of her; it was an angel with a fiery sword who put them both out of God's Eden, she remembered. But some of Eve's memories must have been self-reproachful, and Emma was spared that misery. She was also a fine enough type to appreciate that.

She was shutting up her little shrine when Jerry Black found her. They met with tears that had not started at their meeting; for Jerry had wept at having to return in sorrow to the house where but yesterday hope had hurried him.

To begin a new series of troubles just as he had completed an old one told on his nerves. He had spent the long night praying for Emma, his head on his shiny rosewood dining table.

He always showed this table with pride; it was made from the extra wood he had been commissioned to buy for the Bentley coffins. He had made it himself, and time and again had shown it to Miss Bentley, in whom he felt a great disappointment, as she never manifested any satisfaction at the sight. The cats leaped upon it nightly, as it was Jerry's habitual place of prayer, and it sometimes seemed to him that they exchanged glances with each other in his despite, glances of criticism at his fervour. He never drove them away, however.

"Emma," he said, his lips trembling and his pale eyes filling fast, "your trouble's fearful heavy, but you won't give in. I've seen to Quarry, and it jest ain't no use; you can't get anything out of him; he give it all in to the Workers' Protective Circle. He give it in to the aggression fund. They're going to order a strike for the same pay for winter days nine hours' work, as they get for a ten-hours' summer's day. I think that's it. My work's among the peaceful, and sometimes I thank God I hev it mostly among dead men, seein' what the live ones is like. But, Emma, he's give the money in, so's the strike fund can grow. He's a gainin', winnin' kind of speaker, and he's give up what he took to their cause, and no one ain't a-goin' to touch him. Now you jest remember that the night's blackest just before the sun comes, and don't you loose your grip. When Jarlsen comes out from the blast you want him to find you jest es straight and steady es when he was took—don't you now?"

The tears slipped from Emma's eyes at the little man's tone. Her face was as tranquil as it was sorrowing, and, as she answered, there was no bitterness in her voice and no fretfulness or rebellion in gesture or look. She did not feel bound to exhibit spirit in his presence. "O Jerry," she said, "I think I do. But I can't stay fit for him when I live with thieves who rob him. I'm glad he got the blast ef I have to get low-toned; he'll be nearer a mate for me."

Jerry stayed on and helped her. He packed away the white dress; he was used to handling things that were sacred to the memory of a happy past, and began to pull Emma's house to pieces as only a woman could be expected to do. Martha Long came in; she was sewing as she walked. She was a brisk woman, and got through half her work on the wing.

"God's name!" she said to Black, "what's come to Emma? She looks hurt, and white as a death-sheet."

Jerry told her what had happened, and Martha, without a word, went over and took both the girl's hands in hers and pressed them to her sides; she never lost hold of her sewing, and presently set to work again.

"Well," she half screamed in indignation, "of all the poison toads and irregular vipers in the world and out of it, I guess Quarry's the lowest down. He's a dirt-mean man! I suppose you'll move out, and take the yeller house on the Pastures. There ain't no one in it since last May, and it has a porch. You won't stay there long," Martha said with conviction. "Your kind don't keep to no rent-free Stonepastures. You'll come back to the town, and the crowd'll cheer you— you'll see."

"Well," Emma replied, "I'm going this afternoon."

Accordingly, at five, or a little later, Jerry brought a funeral carriage By the Bridge, and old Butte and Emma and Jerry and Martha carried Jarlsen on a shake-down along the Tracks. The sun, as Jerry observed, was "leanin' pretty near the west line," and the sky was bright above the Stonepastures. It had cleared in the early afternoon, and all the odours, bad and good, seemed flying about, riding on the cool breezes that swept over the Tracks. The high-standing ripe grasses caught the level shafts of sun and bowed before the wind, glorified in the bright light. Jarlsen questioned them about his removal, but gave no evidence that he heard their replies except once, when he said that Emma "sounded" tired. But his voice died away in groanings, and he could not answer their other questions. Emma felt that he heard her voice and did not distinguish the words.

Jerry felt so too. He reminded Emma of the blind man in the Testament. "He seen the men first as trees," he said, "even when he was cured with grace, and not with herbs and ointment and such; he didn't get clear vision right away."

Emma felt happier than she had thought possible. She ran back into the yard and slipped off her shoe. "I'll get the favour of home for him," she thought.

But while the handful of mould was still in her hand she put her shoe on again. "I'd liefer shake off the dust from my feet," she said; "this ain't no home to get the favour from."

Martha Long stood at the gate, "You're in a hurry to go," she remarked.

"To-morrow begins the new month's rent," said Emma. "I quit to-day or pay to-morrow. I'm goin' where there ain't no rents to pay. I can't afford rents and city doctors together."

Martha's face darkened. "I'm layin' for him right here," she called as the funeral carriage moved away.

She was surprised at Emma's goodbye mood; it was so resolute and cheerful. "He's a pretty low reptile," was the last thing she called to Emma as the conveyance grew smaller on the distant road.

X.

QUARRY RECKONS WITHOUT HIS HOSTESS.

"Strife's a poor thing to come home to."

IN two days' time Emma was "settled in." Hers was an odd house for the Stonepastures. She paid no rent for it, but there were curtains at the windows and a shoe-scraper and a mat at the door. She had not been up an hour on her first morning before the grass around the house was cut down with a borrowed sickle. The objectless, listless denizens of the district watched her with some pleasure. They had no individual life, merely existing as a class and watching the individuality of others take shape in thrift and then in prosperity with a dull envy. One man said she "hed a peck of ambition" in a tone that meant on the Pastures, in " Calamity Row," that any endeavour to better one's self comes to confusion.

At first the big boulders depressed her somewhat, but Jerry told her she could " garden on them " in the summer time; and, indeed, flowers could grow from the thin soil that edged them. For two weeks and more she lived, quietly amazed to find herself so happy. From day to day she watched the Swede's improvement. As the pain

Quarry Reckons. 137

left him he took to singing, but his voice was not so accurate as in the old days when he heard clearly. Many of the songs she had heard from him in courting time, and she was infinitely happy to know that he remembered them as well as she did. He would tell the meaning of each verse after he had sung it, as she cooked or sewed after shaving all day.

For she shaved again. It seemed very odd and yet very natural to her. She had a good deal of business to arrange before "resuming trade." Her subscriptions to the Philadelphia Ledger and the Workfellows' Union had run out; in fact, her wedding day had been dependent on their expiration. Emma had a great idea of doing things the right way, and news has been the tradition of barber-shops since men's vanity first devised a shorn chin.

Emma was gratified to find her standing unimpaired by her sojourn with the paupers. Socially she seemed secure. The women were prone to be officiously sympathetic, and were also inclined to disbelieve the tale of Quarry's misdeed. "There's faults on both sides, maybe," and "Who can see the whole show through a slit in the tent?" were felt to be convenient phrases and used largely as such. The phrase "rent-free" found its way from the neighbours' lips to Emma's ears rather oftener than she cared for; it spurred her on to grudge herself food and deny herself the midday beer it had been her wont to consume. She worked from eight in the morning to six at night, with nothing but bread and soup at her slack time in the early afternoon.

The soup was much like Quarry's stories — made up out of almost nothing. She carried it to work in a bottle with a screwed-on tin top; this she put into the little boiler that the shaving water was heated in, "and so," she would say, to amuse a new customer, "thet's all the cooking I hev to do; I boil my bottle, and there I am!"

She had rented a room By the Bridge from Miss Bentley, who was much surprised when Emma paid the rent; and through her new and improved business situation in the town she was able to command a "high-class custom."

Since the evening that Quarry had suggested the depot as a place of residence Emma had been free of his presence. She had heard of him from the men, however, and knew that he was speaking to them from the Bridge every evening. Revolt was in the air of Soot City; there were meetings, quite covertly, conducted by socialistic workmen in the cause of workfellows' profits. Monopoly and co-operative profit were talked of constantly, and Grigg sold many drinks. It is a pity that the workingmen who invent Utopias should attempt to sanctify them with an alcoholic immersion. It antagonizes even the fair-minded. The preachers took to finding comparisons, more or less apposite, between Dives and Lazarus, pronouncing the socialism of him who has not, grabbing from him who has, to be merely a modern variation of a scriptural scheme of all things in common. As some men go to church to find biblical sanction for their shortcomings; the ringleaders of what was fast becoming an agitation, took to the sanctuaries, whither the rest of the town felt it safe to follow them.

Emma regarded Quarry's effrontery as monumental, but she never conceived a possibility of his coming to her new house in the Stonepastures. She felt that, as she had gone down in the world, he thought he had risen, and that the Stonepastures were very far away from him now. Her eyes would scan the road, in her swift evening walks searching for his slightly crooked form. The thought of him distressed her, as horror comes upon a child in the dark, and after nightfall she remembered him as such a power for evil. Returning from the town she always wore for warmth her leathern apron with a shawl, her jacket was too good to be worn out in the dark. This scruple was pure conscience, for she no longer had Jarlsen's eye for which to save her dresses.

He could tell the difference in

footfalls now, and distinguish voices. Emma longed for the moment when he should be able to hear her speak his name. This hoped-for moment occupied many of her hours, and she thought of it on the still, cold night when she saw Quarry walking toward the Pastures about ten yards ahead of her. She slackened her pace instantly, and he was soon lost in the starless dark.

She dreaded him. As she walked she feared she might stumble on him lying drunk in her path, with his mouth full of the hideous words he used at such times; or, this fear forgotten, her breath would come in loud pantings at the thought of his hands laid on her from behind. When she came to her own door there was still no sight of him; she looked both up and down the road to make sure. She could not see far, for most of the houses were dark; lights are too expensive for the rent-free Pastures. Raising the latch, she pushed the door quietly open and looked into her own home.

Quarry was at the kitchen table facing her, glaring in Jarlsen's serenely blind countenance. Sleep had double-locked the Swede's seared vision, and in complete unconsciousness he breathed freely, within a glance of Quarry's eyes alive with malice.

Emma was frightened, so much so that she could not call. It seemed that Quarry must have something to kill with, in his coarse, cramped hands. It flashed across her that if she received him roughly he would strike or stab, and that an appearance of politeness would surely gain her time. Calmness came to her when she had determined how to act.

She rattled the latch, her heart jumping so that she felt as if it had thrown her into the room. Quarry let fall something that gave out the sound of thin metal as it struck the brick flooring round the stove. A flight of chills froze her blood, while her cheeks burned with a steady, excited glow.

Quarry could not avoid her eyes and she saw that were he to have the first word he would announce himself at bay and make trouble. She almost ran to him with her hand stretched out. "Quarry," said she in a little voice that she strained to make audible, "Quarry, you'll have a bite, won't you? It's a cold bite, but a ready one."

Emma thought later that it was at the sound of Quarry's name in her voice that Jarlsen wakened. He knew at once that Quarry was there, for a look that had been absent from his face since they moved from By the Tracks swept its strong patience and sweetness away. He stood on his feet and reached out for the Englishman. The bandages on his right hand seemed too tight, and the veins in it bursting.

"I'm not dead yet!" he said

fiercely, "and no thanks to you!"

Emma could have cried for joy. To her it seemed more than likely that he saw again; but when she noticed how easily Quarry had eluded his big rival, the situation was obscured.

"Did I hurt him?" called Jarlsen eagerly. He had fallen back on his chair, but was sitting on its edge, his eyes burning, and the blood reddening the fine skin on his forehead.

She did not answer, having learned not to waste words on his deafness. She saw Quarry stoop down and lift up the knife he had let fall.

Then she spoke, and very gently.

"You'd better stay here, Quarry," she said; "you're accustomed to your home here, and there's most sleep in an old nest."

And he stayed. Emma turned him in with old Butte, and lighted a new candle, which she left to illumine the rats through the night. Then she locked Jarlsen's door on the outside, and tied the key around her neck. She reflected with pride that her Swede had only been sitting up for two days, and yet wanted to fight on the evening of the second. In her joy at his returning strength she lost sight of danger.

XI.

THE STRIKE.

"Having ears to hear, let them hear."

THE sleep of young strength puts a wide distance between yesterday's cares and to-day's. The dawn that awoke Emma was gray, but it did not suggest the blight of ashes as had last night's twilight. She was sure of the return of Jarlsen's faculties, and she also knew that Quarry could have made no disturbance through the night. She was inclined to think that he meant to frighten them, and by daylight his acts seemed more like very bad manners than like an attempt at murder.

In the morning, before setting out, she changed the bandage on Jarlsen's hand. The wide burns were "guttering," seaming up in red lines. She told him this, and though he made no reply she felt sure, with unshakable, feminine sureness, that he had heard. She led him out to his hammock and placed him in it. Quarry was haranguing Old Butte, and the sound of his voice seemed to make the Swede nervous. Emma was certain that he had heard him.

She had always liked the Pastures as a place to walk; the air was less flat than in the town; and it was pleasant to set one's face against poverty and one's feet toward a place where people were rich enough to pay rent. Bentley's Place overtopped the city on an artificial and costly eminence. The little house that was placed like a lodge was the terminal station of the narrow-gauge railway. She knew herself to be two miles and three quarters from that, and a mile or more from the plant.

Usually she met the day squad coming out from the town, the men standing in the ore cars, the smoke from their pipes and the straining, overworked little engine blown behind them toward the town—like a message sent home, Emma thought. But to-day no cars passed, and she, being a child of toil, was quick to know that this meant a strike. She hurried on to her earnings, remembering that when men are out of work they have all day in which to spend their savings. Women see so little in strikes but higher wages until some one is dead.

When she reached the Bridge it was crowded with people. Men who had not worked at the plant for years were exhorting their fellows not to submit to tyranny. Many large words were being misused with great pride by those who never had a chance to talk except when the crowd was too busy to listen. The women were not very carefully dressed, having had no time for fastenings or strings. They, together with the children they brought with them, seemed to regard the occasion as one of festivity.

Nothing was denounced very definitely. One stranger was said to be a reporter, whereupon half a dozen people beset him, anxious to have their views in the paper. Emma could learn nothing from any of them. They used Quarry's and Bowa's names frequently, so that she forebore mentioning under whose roof the Englishman had passed the night.

Her shop was in the fourth house from the Bridge; a steep diagonal path ran from its back door to the Tracks. The men were swarming to it before she was quite ready to have them, and many arrived by the rarely used footway. News came with them, and she found herself believing first one report and then another. Bowa came to be shaved; she was surprised at his thinking of a thing so incidental to a holiday toilet as a shave, but she supposed that he was resolved to die tidy, and said as much.

He could not be at the plant, he explained, and felt that he had no need to be there. His smile was exceedingly subtle, but his hands worked against his will in an embarrassed fashion.

The day wore on until about four o'clock. Her business had been immense, and she had listened to the many accounts and descriptions of the plant until she felt she knew it perfectly. In the centre was the powder house, where explosives were kept; on the city flank was the nutt and bolt factory, and very near, but south of it, the furnace. It was set on a steep "slide" of rock; its door, through which the furnace was fed, was on the summit side; and on the base side, lower on the slide by eight feet or more, was another door through which the "cinder" flew away at night into the darkness like a burning river. This door seems complicated on paper, though in fact its construction is simple. A skewer secures it at its upper edge—a skewer with a large loop at one end. Into this loop the hook of the fire-tenders' strange implement is thrust when the door is to be opened. "The Devil's Crook" is what the men have named the long oak stick finished at one end with an iron hook. It does look like a thing wherewith to herd black sheep.

Emma was weary of constant exclamation and argument. It was time she ate; so she closed her door and "boiled her bottle," allowing the men who were already in the shop to remain there. She saw Bowa get up from his chair and leave by the back door, silent and hurried. As was natural, Emma turned to the window to see what had caught his eye in the street.

Young Bentley had driven up in

his buggy; his liveried servant sat beside him, and the horse he drove plunged and shook with nervousness at being surrounded by a crowd of loud-voiced people. Bentley stood up in the little buggy, having given the reins to his man. "See here," he said, addressing the crowd, "if we have a strike, you'd better remember that I can stand it, and you can't. I've sent police to the plant to protect my property, and you had better stand by them; for the plant is the machine you make your bread with, and it's the only thing you can work at. I've got lots of irons on the fire. Now some one has trifled with this road bed, in the cut here, By the Bridge. I suppose you want to make me lose my charter. I'm going to examine the damage now, and I hope you'll come with me."

He jumped to the ground and began to descend the steps leading to the road-bed in the cut, over which the Bridge is. No one followed him, but with admirable nerve he neither hesitated nor quickened his pace.

Emma remembered that Jarlsen had liked him, and that he had called to ask for him once By the Tracks and twice on the Pastures. No Bentley had visited the Pastures before, and Emma felt the distinction keenly. She opened the door and went out, merely observing to the bystanders that they "hed no spring."

Before she got to the stair's head about six men had followed her, looking deeply ashamed of each other, but at present firm in their duty. Emma let them pass her, and slipped into the advancing crowd.

Bowa and three companions were standing on the tracks by two overturned ore cars. They seemed more sheepish than defiant, and Emma noticed with pride how neat Bowa looked as he tried not to flinch under Bentley's contemptuous gaze. The rails were torn up for about twenty yards, and in the silence that preceded Bentley's first words Emma realized that this meant prison.

"Did you do that?" he said at

length. Then turning to the men at his back, he said very pleasantly, "I think we can put this right with"—his voice grew suddenly louder—"two more to help us."

Two Soot City police appeared, and very quietly secured Bowa and his friends. They were too surprised to make any resistance, and went silent and sullen at Bentley's curt bidding. Some one cried, "Shame!" at the plant owner. Martha Long answered "Nonsense!" very loud. But her tears fell for Bowa, and she pleaded for him in words.

"Mr. Bentley," she said, "he was put up to that. He's young for the shadder of a prison to fall on him. He's as mild as new milk, and he's had his taste, and he won't want no more."

"Martha," Bentley answered, "I think making an example of a workman is making a martyr of him and an enemy of his labour organization. I don't want any strikes, so I'll probably let him off; but I wouldn't promise any one."

Martha went away well comforted, and Emma, when the darkness had fallen, set out for home. She considered the strike was over, and laughed as she made herself pictures of Quarry's discomfiture; his plans would be henceforth unheeded, and, as he had not succeeded, the men would not fear him, and not fearing meant, under such conditions, shunning. She had had a diverting day; the silver jingled in her pocket, and her wish was that Jarlsen might have ears to hear all about it.

The cottage was dark, but before she came within a hundred yards of it, while it yet stood out black and square against the dark east, she heard Jarlsen calling, "Emma, hurry, girl!—Emma, girl, hurry!"

She ran to him, stumbling and in dread, and groped in the darkness of the room with tender hands that feared—she longed to know just what.

"I'm all right," he said; "but listen. Speak to me; I can hear. I've heard ever since we moved. I've wanted to say so, but I wanted to go on hearing your father talk to Quarry. I've heard it all. I'm done with secrets; I'm pretty near done with theirs. Speak to me, Emma; I can prove it."

"I'm so bursting-out happy, I can't talk much," said she.

Her speech followed her in his voice. "'I'm so bursting-out happy, I can't talk much.' But I can hear! Emma, Quarry and your poppa have been setting it up since we came here, and I was afraid to say I heard, for fear two couldn't keep a secret. Emma, we want the plant's pension, and we're going to get it!

"You're going now," he said, "to run out to the plant—to run your best; when you get there, go to the furnace. If you keep right on By the Tracks, nobody'll mind you. Quarry's bought the furnace-minders, and they're going to leave for the station to report a disturbance in the factory. The Devil's Crook is in the little house by the furnace; it is by the door. You take it as you pass—no one'll be there—and when you see a light in the factory you open the centre door and make a flare, for the police can't see in the dark. You'll catch 'em; O Emma, hurry! I've got a good chance to fix Quarry, and he didn't warn me of that blast, or I wouldn't be here now. He put his flag behind his back when he saw me come, and I walked right on. Hurry, Emma girl! Don't burn yourself!"

Emma could feel that he wanted to go himself. She caught up her shawl. "Is it the powder house?" she asked.

"For God's sake," he said loudly, "get started! Of course it is!"

She ran out into the wide darkness. She was racing death, and she knew it.

XII.

THE EYE OF GOD.

"And the eye of God shall pierce the lengthy darkness."

EMMA's first thought was of the time that it would take her to get to the plant. Young Bentley had once run a mile under five minutes, and his feat had been in the newspapers; but she could not, of course, count on herself for like speed. She felt that the cinder flare would light up her life's crisis. Jarlsen's excited voice echoed in her mind, and the thought that

Quarry might have saved him with the warning flag, instead of letting him come unchecked on live powder, urged her on the faster. She saw that to-day's attempt at the Tracks was a forced incident, intended to look like the strike's crisis. She remembered her own part in it with laughter.

She was choked with anxiety. It seemed to her that if the powder house were fired there would be no food anywhere in Soot City. Who would be killed and how much would be damaged was an unanswerable question that weakened her with painful suspense. She barely noticed the hissing rush of her breath or felt the pain in her side. Her feet grew heavy, and the noise of their fall on the road-bed sounded to her as if it was far off in the town. Her neck was craned in the direction of the plant, and she wanted to throw herself along the earth. When the lights at the sidings and at the station grew nearer her dimmed eyes could barely distinguish them. Some warm thing, with a new taste, crept over her lips. She put up her hand to it, and saw in the light at the first siding that it was blood.

Her body rocked with the push of her heart-beats, and "yet," she thought, "I may be late."

At last she passed the station. Through its blindless windows she could see Benz, the furnace-tender, talking fast to the police. For a moment she thought of going in and telling her story, but she feared a loss of time, and started furiously up the grade to the tool-house. She found the door standing open and entered boldly, snatching the crook and striking at a man who raised himself from the floor. He lay down again at once, saying, "All right, only don't tell me where you put it."

"I'm in time," she thought.

There was a little patch of light before the threshold. Looking up, she saw four policemen crossing by the powder house to the factory. Then the scheme came entire into her puzzled brain. They were called out on search and it was their lights in the factory that were to be taken as the signal for Quarry's men to fire the mine. The furnace-tenders had gone as guides, and the unshifted cinder could not expose offenders.

"He's a cute viper!" Emma was talking to herself to keep her nerve; she was spent and breathless.

The heat by the furnace was terrible; it shone on the iron trough in an outlined square of yellow, where the light streamed through the door cracks. She fitted the crook's hook to the loop of the skewer and paused, waiting. Her thoughts were busy with the way in which they might fire the powder stores. Heat and cold hurried through her alternately; her hands and brow were wet. There were, of course, no men on duty at the plant save forty of the factory force, Quarry among them. Emma saw that this was part of the blind.

The electric lights were out; they had not been turned on since early the last evening, but presently one shone from the ground floor of the factory. Emma pulled back her crook exultingly, but the skewer would not give. She jerked, but it was firm. Gathering her strength, she braced her feet and threw herself back. She saw a fiery line pass above her head, and heard the red-hot skewer tinkle against a stone behind her. She rushed to the front of the furnace to get rid of the heat, and stood on the crest of the incline.

As the cinder flew in a glowing mass down the trough to the cinder hill, she saw the spires at the city and the Bridge. Then she looked directly before her.

As the night lifted from the plant yard she saw that some one was running; the figure took on it the red of the brightening furnace waste, and the flame of the torch the runner carried grew white in the rosy glare. The light spread higher, and Emma saw the tops of the elm trees that grew on the other side of the factory. The cinder rattled in the trough with a grating loudness.

"He hes a train of oiled rope laid," said she.

The plant-hand was Quarry, and

still he ran toward the powder house in the vivid light. The men, most of them police, were watching him. He knelt with his light in his hand, and fell forward, the torch under him. Then Emma heard a pistol shot that sounded like snapping fingers in the din of the cinder waste.

Bentley's voice was hardly heard in the various noise that followed the shot. "Lock up God's eye!" he called; "it's done big work, but don't waste fuel."

And a woman's voice, peevish from fatigue, called from the height: "I can't—I'm broken, I'm so tired!"

But Quarry did not stir; his torch was out. And in the house on the Pastures Jarlsen's eyes strained themselves to pierce their own darkness, although the cloudy sky was like a red sea, and the plant stood out plainly with orange elm trees and bright roofs.

EPILOGUE.

WE were disputing in the train as to whether it was five or six years since Quarry's death. I said six, and was told that I was always wrong. My adversary evidently considered this second-rate rejoinder a retort. Presently he said, "You may be right, for I think Jarlsen's boy is five."

Jerry Black met us at the station; he wore a bailiff's uniform of corduroy. The Bentleys were very English now, but kinder than ever. We got into an omnibus, and asked Jerry to come too. He had to be urged, for he is still modest.

"How are the Stonepastures?" said I, anxious to start the conversation.

"Lean livin' yet," he answered, sighing; "but we've got a home for the aged indigent, and a hospital."

He began to talk in earnest, and, among other things, told us that Emma paid the doctor the week after Quarry died. He said she felt as if she had killed Quarry, but that her marriage had put it out of her head. "The Jarlsens are getting on fine," he remarked confidentially, "more than happy in their fortunes. August has sold his idea for freight couplers to the plant, and he's living in the back of the new schoolhouse, and he goes away singing and gets paid for it. He bought a piano with his savings."

"Emma's too fine to shave me, I suppose," said I.

"Don't name it to her, please," implored Jerry.

We arrived at the church—it was Bentley's wedding we were attending—and on either side of the walk through the yard the men and women of the plant waited for the bride. There was not a foot of space left in the church. Bowa stood next me, and with him was Martha Long. "It's a pleasanter time than the last," she said as I greeted her. We had been staying at the plant in the strike when Quarry had gone under, and I was pleased that she remembered it. Black was everywhere. At last he pushed us all back to clear the path for the bride. Bentley was in the church at the chancel.

Then there broke on our eager ears the finest tenor I had ever heard. They say he sang a Swedish wedding song. I don't care what it was—I almost cried when he stopped. His voice rose high and strong, and seemed to spread like perfume; he sang gladly.

"Who is that?" I asked.

Every one within hearing answered proudly, "Jarlsen."

THE END.

D. APPLETON & CO.'S PUBLICATIONS.

AN IMAGINATIVE MAN. By ROBERT S. HICH-ENS, author of "The Green Carnation." 12mo. Cloth, $1.25.

"One of the brightest books of the year."—*Boston Budget.*

"Altogether delightful, fascinating, unusual."—*Cleveland Amusement Gazette.*

"A study in character. . . . Just as entertaining as though it were the conventional story of love and marriage. The clever hand of the author of 'The Green Carnation' is easily detected in the caustic wit and pointed epigram."—*Jeannette L. Gilder, in the New York World.*

MASTER AND MAN. By Count LEO TOLSTOY. 16mo. Cloth, 75 cents.

"Crowded with these characteristic touches which mark his literary work."—*Public Opinion.*

"From the very start the reader feels that it is from a master's pen."—*Boston Times.*

"Reveals a wonderful knowledge of the workings of the human mind, and it tells a tale that not only stirs the emotions, but gives us a better insight into our own hearts."—*San Francisco Argonaut.*

THE ZEIT-GEIST. By L. DOUGALL, author of "The Mermaid," "Beggars All," etc. 16mo. Cloth, 75 cents.

"It is impossible for one to read it without feeling better for having done so; without having a desire to aid his fellow-men."—*New York Times.*

"One of the best of the short stories of the day."—*Boston Journal.*

"One of the most remarkable novels of the year."—*New York Commercial Advertiser.*

"Powerful in conception, treatment, and influence."—*Boston Globe.*

THE LAND OF THE SUN. Vistas Mexicanas. By CHRISTIAN REID, author of "The Land of the Sky," "A Comedy of Elopement," etc. Illustrated. 12mo. Cloth, $1.75.

"Perhaps no book of recent date gives a simpler and at the same time more effective picture of this truly beautiful 'land of the sun' than is to be found in this striking volume."—*St. Louis Republic.*

"One of the most charming books of travel that we have read for a long time. . . . Certainly no one should ever think of visiting Mexico without taking this book of splendid description and delightful romance with him."—*Boston Home Journal.*

"He who would see the grandeurs of Mexico through the eyes of another should give careful perusal to Christian Reid's portrayal of 'The Land of the Sun,' which in every detail is a fitting tribute to the past, present, and future conditions of the new Spain."—*Chicago Evening Post.*

New York: D. APPLETON & CO., 72 Fifth Avenue.

D. APPLETON & CO.'S PUBLICATIONS.

A STREET IN SUBURBIA. By EDWIN PUGH. 12mo. Cloth, $1.00.

"Simplicity of style, strength, and delicacy of character study will mark this book as one of the most significant of the year."—*New York Press.*

"Thoroughly entertaining, and more—it shows traces of a creative genius something akin to Dickens."—*Boston Traveler.*

"In many respects the best of all the books of lighter literature brought out this season."—*Providence News.*

"A clever series of character sketches."—*Elmira Telegram.*

"Rippling over from end to end with fun and humor."—*London Academy.*

MAJESTY. A Novel. By LOUIS COUPERUS. Translated by A. TEIXEIRA DE MATTOS and ERNEST DOWSON. 12mo. Cloth, $1.00.

"No novelist whom we can call to mind has ever given the world such a masterpiece of royal portraiture as Louis Couperus's striking romance entitled 'Majesty.'"—*Philadelphia Record.*

"A very powerful and cleverly written romance."—*New York Times.*

"There is not an uninteresting page in the book, and it ought to be read by all who desire to keep in line with the best that is published in modern fiction."—*Buffalo Commercial.*

THE NEW MOON. By C. E. RAIMOND, author of "George Mandeville's Husband," etc. 12mo. Cloth, $1.00.

"A delicate pathos makes itself felt as the narrative progresses, whose cadences fall on the spirit's consciousness with a sweet and soothing influence not to be measured in words."—*Boston Courier.*

"One of the most impressive of recent works of fiction, both for its matter and especially for its presentation."—*Milwaukee Journal.*

"The story is most graphically told, the characters are admirably drawn, and the moral of the whole thing is very desirable as inculcating an important lesson."—*Chicago Journal.*

"A surprisingly clever book in its way, being direct and simple, and true on every page to the author's purpose."—*New York Times.*

THE WISH. A Novel. By HERMANN SUDERMANN. With a Biographical Introduction by ELIZABETH LEE. 12mo. Cloth, $1.00.

"Contains some superb specimens of original thought."—*New York World.*

"The style is direct and incisive, and holds the unflagging attention of the reader."—*Boston Journal.*

"A powerful story, very simple, very direct."—*Chicago Evening Post.*

New York: D. APPLETON & CO., 72 Fifth Avenue.

S. R. CROCKETT'S LATEST BOOKS.

UNIFORM EDITION. EACH, 12MO. CLOTH, $1.50.

BOG-MYRTLE AND PEAT.

"Here are idyls, epics, dramas of human life, written in words that thrill and burn. . . . Each is a poem that has an immortal flavor. They are fragments of the author's early dreams, too bright, too gorgeous, too full of the blood of rubies and the life of diamonds to be caught and held palpitating in expression's grasp."—*Boston Courier.*

"Contains some of the most dramatic pieces Mr. Crockett has yet written, and in these picturesque sketches he is altogether delightful. . . . The volume is well worth reading—all of it."—*Philadelphia Press.*

"Hardly a sketch among them all that will not afford pleasure to the reader for its genial humor, artistic local coloring, and admirable portrayal of character."—*Boston Home Journal.*

"One dips into the book anywhere and reads on and on, fascinated by the writer's charm of manner."—*Minneapolis Tribune.*

"These stories are lively and vigorous, and have many touches of human nature in them—such touches as we are used to from having read 'The Stickit Minister' and 'The Lilac Sunbonnet.'"—*New Haven Register.*

"'Bog-Myrtle and Peat' contains stories which could only have been written by a man of genius."—*London Chronicle.*

THE LILAC SUNBONNET. A Love Story.

"A love story pure and simple, one of the old-fashioned, wholesome, sunshiny kind, with a pure-minded, sound-hearted hero, and a heroine who is merely a good and beautiful woman; and if any other love story half so sweet has been written this year, it has escaped our notice."—*New York Times.*

"A solid novel with an old-time flavor, as refreshing when compared to the average modern story as is a whiff of air from the hills to one just come from a hothouse."—*Boston Beacon.*

"The general conception of the story, the motive of which is the growth of love between the young chief and heroine, is delineated with a sweetness and a freshness, a naturalness and a certainty, which places 'The Lilac Sunbonnet' among the best stories of the time."—*New York Mail and Express.*

"In its own line this little love story can hardly be excelled. It is a pastoral, an idyl—the story of love and courtship and marriage of a fine young man and a lovely girl—no more. But it is told in so thoroughly delightful a manner, with such playful humor, such delicate fancy, such true and sympathetic feeling, that nothing more could be desired."—*Boston Traveller.*

New York: D. APPLETON & CO., 72 Fifth Avenue.

D. APPLETON & CO.'S PUBLICATIONS.

NOVELS BY HALL CAINE.

THE MANXMAN. 12mo. Cloth, $1.50.

"A story of marvelous dramatic intensity, and in its ethical meaning has a force comparable only to Hawthorne's 'Scarlet Letter.'"—*Boston Beacon.*

"A work of power which is another stone added to the foundation of enduring fame to which Mr. Caine is yearly adding."—*Public Opinion.*

"A wonderfully strong study of character; a powerful analysis of those elements which go to make up the strength and weakness of a man, which are at fierce warfare within the same breast; contending against each other, as it were, the one to raise him to fame and power, the other to drag him down to degradation and shame. Never in the whole range of literature have we seen the struggle between these forces for supremacy over the man more powerfully, more realistically delineated than Mr. Caine pictures it."—*Boston Home Journal.*

THE DEEMSTER. A Romance of the Isle of Man. 12mo. Cloth, $1.50.

"Hall Caine has already given us some very strong and fine work, and 'The Deemster' is a story of unusual power. . . . Certain passages and chapters have an intensely dramatic grasp, and hold the fascinated reader with a force rarely excited nowadays in literature."—*The Critic.*

"One of the strongest novels which has appeared in many a day."—*San Francisco Chronicle.*

THE BONDMAN. New edition. 12mo. Cloth, $1.50.

"The welcome given to this story has cheered and touched me, but I am conscious that, to win a reception so warm, such a book must have had readers who brought to it as much as they took away. . . . I have called my story a saga, merely because it follows the epic method, and I must not claim for it at any point the weighty responsibility of history, or serious obligations to the world of fact. But it matters not to me what Icelanders may call 'The Bondman,' if they will honor me by reading it in the open-hearted spirit and with the free mind with which they are content to read of Grettir and of his fights with the Troll."—*From the Author's Preface.*

CAPT'N DAVY'S HONEYMOON. A Manx Yarn. 12mo. Paper, 50 cents; cloth, $1.00.

"A new departure by this author. Unlike his previous works, this little tale is almost wholly humorous, with, however, a current of pathos underneath. It is not always that an author can succeed equally well in tragedy and in comedy, but it looks as though Mr. Hall Caine would be one of the exceptions."—*London Literary World.*

"It is pleasant to meet the author of 'The Deemster' in a brightly humorous little story like this. . . . It shows the same observation of Manx character, and much of the same artistic skill."—*Philadelphia Times.*

New York: D. APPLETON & CO., 72 Fifth Avenue.

By A. CONAN DOYLE.

THE STARK MUNRO LETTERS. Being a Series of Twelve Letters written by J. STARK MUNRO, M. B., to his friend and former fellow-student, Herbert Swanborough, of Lowell, Massachusetts, during the years 1881-1884. Illustrated. 12mo. Buckram, $1.50.

This original and dramatic story presents fresh types, extraordinary situations, and novel suggestions with a freshness and vigor which show that the romancer's heart was in his work. How far certain incidents of the story are based upon personal experiences it is impossible to say, but the unflagging interest and unexpected phases of the romance are no less in evidence than the close personal relations established between author and reader. In the "Stark Munro Letters" the author has achieved another success which will add to the number of his American friends and readers.

"Any one who has read any of the fascinating stories in which the shrewd detective, Sherlock Holmes, figures as the very personification of detective logic applied to the detection of crime, knows that Conan Doyle is a story-teller of the very first order of merit. Like his own character, Sherlock Holmes, he possesses the power of getting out of everything all there is in it."—*Philadelphia Item.*

"Dr. Doyle's stories are so well known for their strong dramatic style, for the elegance of expression, that anything new from his pen is sure to be warmly welcomed. His readers are sure of getting a literary treat from anything he writes. He is broad-minded and liberal, and the man who could write two such books as 'The White Company' and 'The Refugees' has a future which the shades of Scott and Dickens might envy."—*Albany Times-Union.*

ROUND THE RED LAMP. 12mo. Cloth, $1.50. Seventh edition.

The "Red Lamp," the trade-mark, as it were, of the English country practitioner's office, is the central point of these dramatic stories of professional life. There are no secrets for the surgeon, and, a surgeon himself as well as a novelist, the author has made a most artistic use of the motives and springs of action revealed to him in a field of which he is the master.

"Too much can not be said in praise of these strong productions, that, to read, keep one's heart leaping to the throat and the mind in a tumult of anticipation to the end.... No series of short stories in modern literature can approach them."—*Hartford Times.*

"The reading of these choice stories will prove an exciting pleasure to all who may linger on the pages that present them."—*Boston Courier.*

"A strikingly realistic and decidedly original contribution to modern literature."—*Boston Saturday Evening Gazette.*

New York: D. APPLETON & CO., 72 Fifth Avenue.

D. APPLETON & CO.'S PUBLICATIONS.

PAUL AND VIRGINIA. By BERNARDIN DE SAINT-PIERRE. With a Biographical Sketch, and numerous Illustrations by Maurice Leloir. 8vo. Cloth, gilt top, uniform with "Picciola," "The Story of Colette," and "An Attic Philosopher in Paris." $1.50.

It is believed that this standard edition of "Paul and Virginia" with Leloir's charming illustrations will prove a most acceptable addition to the series of illustrated foreign classics in which D. Appleton & Co. have published "The Story of Colette," "An Attic Philosopher in Paris," and "Picciola." No more sympathetic illustrator than Leloir could be found, and his treatment of this masterpiece of French literature invests it with a peculiar value.

PICCIOLA. By X. B. SAINTINE. With 130 Illustrations by J. F. GUELDRY. 8vo. Cloth, gilt top, $1.50.

"Saintine's 'Picciola,' the pathetic tale of the prisoner who raised a flower between the cracks of the flagging of his dungeon, has passed definitely into the list of classic books. . . . It has never been more beautifully housed than in this edition, with its fine typography, binding, and sympathetic illustrations."—*Philadelphia Telegraph.*

AN ATTIC PHILOSOPHER IN PARIS; or, A Peep at the World from a Garret. Being the Journal of a Happy Man. By ÉMILE SOUVESTRE. With numerous Illustrations. 8vo. Cloth, gilt top, $1.50.

"A suitable holiday gift for a friend who appreciates refined literature."—*Boston Times.*

"The influence of the book is wholly good. The volume is a particularly handsome one."—*Philadelphia Telegraph.*

"It is a classic. It has found an appropriate reliquary. Faithfully translated, charmingly illustrated by Jean Claude with full-page pictures, vignettes in the text, and head and tail pieces, printed in graceful type on handsome paper, and bound with an art worthy of Matthews, in half-cloth, ornamented on the cover, it is an exemplary book, fit to be 'a treasure for aye.'"—*New York Times.*

THE STORY OF COLETTE. A new large-paper edition. With 36 Illustrations. 8vo. Cloth, gilt top, $1.50.

"One of the handsomest of the books of fiction for the holiday season."—*Philadelphia Bulletin.*

"One of the gems of the season. . . . It is the story of the life of young womanhood in France, dramatically told, with the light and shade and coloring of the genuine artist, and is utterly free from that which mars too many French novels. In its literary finish it is well nigh perfect, indicating the hand of the master."—*Boston Traveller.*

New York: D. APPLETON & CO., 72 Fifth Avenue.

D. APPLETON & CO.'S PUBLICATIONS.

A FRIEND OF THE QUEEN. (Marie Antoinette—Count de Fersen.) By PAUL GAULOT. With Two Portraits. 12mo. Cloth, $2.00.

"M. Gaulot deserves thanks for presenting the personal history of Count Fersen in a manner so evidently candid and unbiased."—*Philadelphia Bulletin.*

"There are some characters in history of whom we never seem to grow tired. Of no one is this so much the case as of the beautiful Marie Antoinette, and of that life which is at once so eventful and so tragic. . . . In this work we have much that up to the present time has been only vaguely known."—*Philadelphia Press.*

"A historical volume that will be eagerly read."—*New York Observer.*

"One of those captivating recitals of the romance of truth which are the gilding of the pill of history."—*London Daily News.*

"It tells with new and authentic details the romantic story of Count Fersen's (the Friend of the Queen) devotion to Marie Antoinette, of his share in the celebrated flight to Varennes, and in many other well-known episodes of the unhappy Queen's life."—*London Times.*

"If the book had no more recommendation than the mere fact that Marie Antoinette and Count Fersen are rescued at last from the voluminous and contradictory representations with which the literature of that period abounds, it would be enough compensation to any reader to become acquainted with the true delineations of two of the most romantically tragic personalities."—*Boston Globe.*

*T*HE ROMANCE OF AN EMPRESS. Catharine II of Russia. By K. WALISZEWSKI. With Portrait. 12mo. Cloth, $2.00.

"Of Catharine's marvelous career we have in this volume a sympathetic, learned, and picturesque narrative. No royal career, not even of some of the Roman or papal ones, has better shown us how truth can be stranger than fiction."—*New York Times.*

"A striking and able work, deserving of the highest praise."—*Philadelphia Ledger.*

"The book is well called a romance, for, although no legends are admitted in it, and the author has been at pains to present nothing but verified facts, the actual career of the subject was so abnormal and sensational as to seem to belong to fiction."—*New York Sun.*

"A dignified, handsome, indeed superb volume, and well worth careful reading."—*Chicago Herald.*

"It is a most wonderful story, charmingly told, with new material to sustain it, and a breadth and temperance and consideration that go far to soften one's estimate of one of the most extraordinary women of history."—*New York Commercial Advertiser.*

"The perusal of such a book can not fail to add to that breadth of view which is so essential to the student of universal history."—*Philadelphia Bulletin.*

New York: D. APPLETON & CO., 72 Fifth Avenue.

D. APPLETON & CO.'S PUBLICATIONS.

MANY INVENTIONS. By RUDYARD KIPLING. Containing fourteen stories, several of which are now published for the first time, and two poems. 12mo, 427 pages. Cloth, $1.50.

"The reader turns from its pages with the conviction that the author has no superior to-day in animated narrative and virility of style. He remains master of a power in which none of his contemporaries approach him —the ability to select out of countless details the few vital ones which create the finished picture. He knows how, with a phrase or a word, to make you see his characters as he sees them, to make you feel the full meaning of a dramatic situation."—*New York Tribune.*

"'Many Inventions' will confirm Mr. Kipling's reputation. . . . We would cite with pleasure sentences from almost every page, and extract incidents from almost every story. But to what end? Here is the completest book that Mr. Kipling has yet given us in workmanship, the weightiest and most humane in breadth of view."—*Pall Mall Gazette.*

"Mr. Kipling's powers as a story-teller are evidently not diminishing. We advise everybody to buy 'Many Inventions,' and to profit by some of the best entertainment that modern fiction has to offer."—*New York Sun.*

"'Many Inventions' will be welcomed wherever the English language is spoken. . . . Every one of the stories bears the imprint of a master who conjures up incident as if by magic, and who portrays character, scenery, and feeling with an ease which is only exceeded by the boldness of force." —*Boston Globe.*

"The book will get and hold the closest attention of the reader." —*American Bookseller.*

"Mr. Rudyard Kipling's place in the world of letters is unique. He sits quite aloof and alone, the incomparable and inimitable master of the exquisitely fine art of short-story writing. Mr. Robert Louis Stevenson has perhaps written several tales which match the run of Mr. Kipling's work, but the best of Mr. Kipling's tales are matchless, and his latest collection, 'Many Inventions,' contains several such."—*Philadelphia Press.*

"Of late essays in fiction the work of Kipling can be compared to only three—Blackmore's 'Lorna Doone,' Stevenson's marvelous sketch of Villon in the 'New Arabian Nights,' and Thomas Hardy's 'Tess of the D'Urbervilles.' . . . It is probably owing to this extreme care that 'Many Inventions' is undoubtedly Mr. Kipling's best book."—*Chicago Post.*

"Mr. Kipling's style is too well known to American readers to require introduction, but it can scarcely be amiss to say there is not a story in this collection that does not more than repay a perusal of them all."—*Baltimore American.*

"As a writer of short stories Rudyard Kipling is a genius. He has had imitators, but they have not been successful in dimming the luster of his achievements by contrast. . . . 'Many Inventions' is the title. And they are inventions—entirely original in incident, ingenious in plot, and startling by their boldness and force."—*Rochester Herald.*

New York: D. APPLETON & CO., 72 Fifth Avenue.

www.ingramcontent.com/pod-product-compliance
Lightning Source LLC
Chambersburg PA
CBHW020847160426
43192CB00007B/817